The Complete Guitar Player Tablature Book

by Russ Shipton

Order No. AM62902
This book © Copyright 1987 Hal Leonard

Designed by Alison Fenton.
Cover photography by Ralph Hall.
Arranged and compiled by Russ Shipton.

Printed in the EU

ISBN: 978-0-7119-0906-9

Visit Hal Leonard Online at
www.halleonard.com

Contact us:
Hal Leonard
7777 West Bluemound Road
Milwaukee, WI 53213
Email: info@halleonard.com

In Europe, contact:
Hal Leonard Europe Limited
42 Wigmore Street
Marylebone, London, W1U 2RY
Email: info@halleonardeurope.com

In Australia, contact:
Hal Leonard Australia Pty. Ltd.
4 Lentara Court
Cheltenham, Victoria, 3192 Australia
Email: info@halleonard.com.au

The tablature in this book does two main things. Like other tablature, it gives you the precise location of the notes on the guitar strings, but by dividing it up into bars and putting beat indications beneath, it also provides sufficient rhythm information for the reader to interpret it easily.

Most solo guitar music comes down to crotchets and quavers, as you can see from the sample bar below with its equivalent in standard music notation:

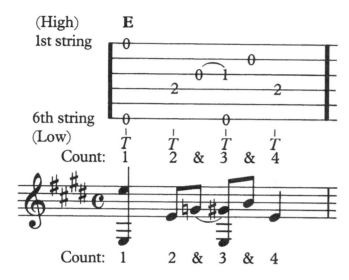

Beat indications beneath the tablature show the rhythm clearly. When there is a note on the beat and no note before the next beat, it will be a crotchet in standard music notation (i.e. the first note in the example above). When two notes are involved, on and then off the beat, these will be like two quavers in music notation. Read the tablature like the standard music notation from left to right and follow the count shown beneath.

Unless a 'swing' rhythm is involved, the notes between beats will be played **exactly** halfway between the beats. The beat notes themselves are of course equally spaced. For information on the swing rhythm, see my notes on the following page.

Here are some guidelines for reading the tablature in this book:

a. The 6 lines represent the 6 strings of the guitar. The thinnest (**high e**) string is at the top, and the thickest (**low e**) at the bottom. Like standard notation, higher notes are higher up the page, and lower notes lower down.

b. Play from left to right like standard music notation, and when notes are vertically in line they should be sounded at the same time. (See my note on embellishments onto the beat on the next page).

c. The letter above the tablature indicates the main chord involved at that point of the accompaniment. Often the most common shape of the chord will be fingered, but not always.

d. The numbers on the strings indicate the string and fret positions for the notes to be played. 'O' means the open string is played, while '1' means the 1st fret is fingered and played. '2' means the 2nd fret, and so on.

e. The **E** chord example opposite begins with two open strings (1st and 6th) played at the same time. The *T* beneath the beats means that the right hand thumb is used. All other notes will be struck by the right hand fingers. Thus the right hand thumb plays the open 6th string at the same time as a right hand finger plays the open 1st string (in a 'pinch' action). These notes are followed by the 2nd fret note on the 4th string. This falls on the 2nd beat of the bar and is played by the right hand thumb. Normally the usual **E** chord shape is held, so the 3rd finger on the left hand will be on the 2nd fret of the 4th string.

Left Hand Fingering

Suggested left hand positions are shown in the photos. Additional fingerings are dealt with in my notes before each piece. Always experiment with your own fingering as well and do what you feel comfortable with.

Right Hand Fingering

As mentioned above, the right hand thumb indications are given beneath the tablature. If the pattern of the thumb strikes remain constant, only the first bar or two will be marked. Usually the right hand thumb plays the three bass strings, and the fingers play the treble strings – the index finger takes the 3rd string, the middle finger the 2nd string and the ring finger the 1st string. Don't worry about breaking these rules sometimes – in the alternating thumb style, for example, the index and middle fingers are often sufficient.

Embellishments

Because various effects can be done on the guitar, special signs have been devised to represent them:

Strum

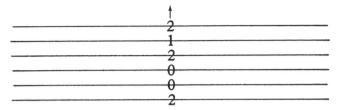

Where the finger(s) or flatpick brushes across some or all of the strings, the appropriate fret indications are given plus an arrow above the tablature. The arrow going up the page is actually a downstrum because the strum is moving from the bass to treble strings.

Hammer-On And Pull-Off

These important embellishments are performed by the left hand after the right hand has struck, and are indicated by the same sign. The left hand finger comes down firmly onto a higher fret for the hammer-on, and comes off a higher fret to a lower one (or open string) for a pull-off. The pull-off has its name because the finger bends the string slightly before coming off. In both cases a second note is produced by the left hand.

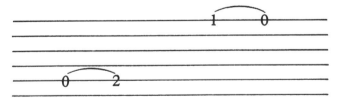

Wow, Slide And Harmonic

These are used less frequently, but are important embellishments.

The wows (bends) on the treble strings are done by pushing the string towards the bass strings. Those on the bass strings mean pushing the string the other way. The slide can of course be up or down, with the left hand finger sliding from one fret to another, producing a second note. The harmonic is indicated by a small dot next to the fret number. The left hand finger must be held lightly on and directly over the fret wire itself for the harmonic note to be produced.

Slap

The right hand fingers come down on to all the strings to produce a 'tap' sound as well as damping the strings. This is the key element of the 'slap style'.

Spread Strum And Quick Arpeggio

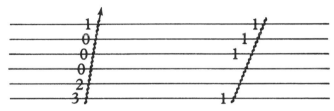

When a strum is done more slowly and deliberately it is marked with a 'wavy' arrow. The same kind of sign is used for a quick arpeggio done with the right hand thumb and three fingers, but without the arrow head.

The Swing Rhythm

Some accompaniments must be 'Swing' – notes or strums between beats are delayed slightly so they are **played nearer the following beat** – unlike the 'straight rhythm' accompaniments, where notes between beats are played exactly halfway between. In this book the following songs involve a swing rhythm: Lucille (only slight), Canadian Hornpipe, Sixteen Tons, Georgia On My Mind, Crumble Blues, Ain't Misbehavin' and Everything Put Together Falls Apart.

Imagine

John Lennon

This great song by John Lennon works well with an arpeggio accompaniment. The chords are straightforward and the right hand thumb plays the notes on the three bass strings while the 1st, 2nd and 3rd strings are played by the ring, middle and index fingers respectively.

The **G** to **C** bass run involves raising the 2nd left hand finger and replacing it, as do the hammer-ons in the **C** and **G** chords. The hammer-on should be quick – the 3rd note in the beat should be played halfway between beats. In musical terms, this means: 

❶ **G** chord

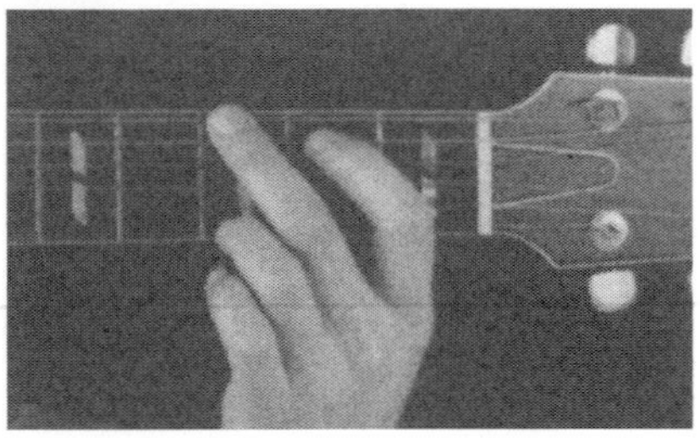

❷ **C** chord

❸ **Em** chord

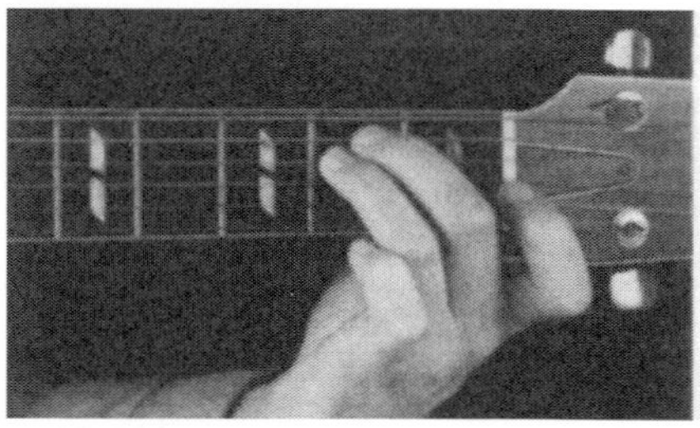

❹ **Am** chord

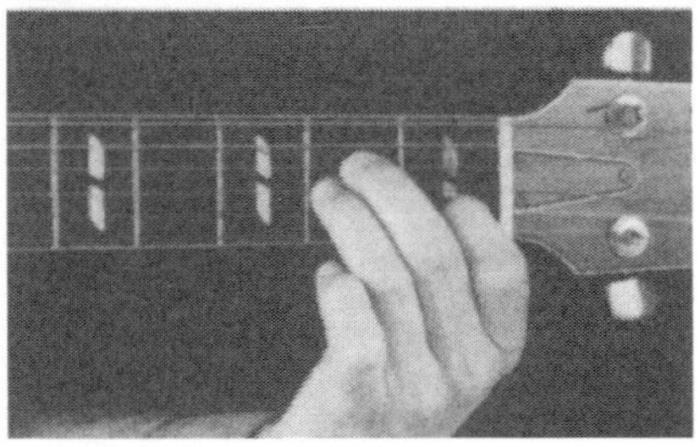

❺ **Am7** chord

❻ **D9** chord

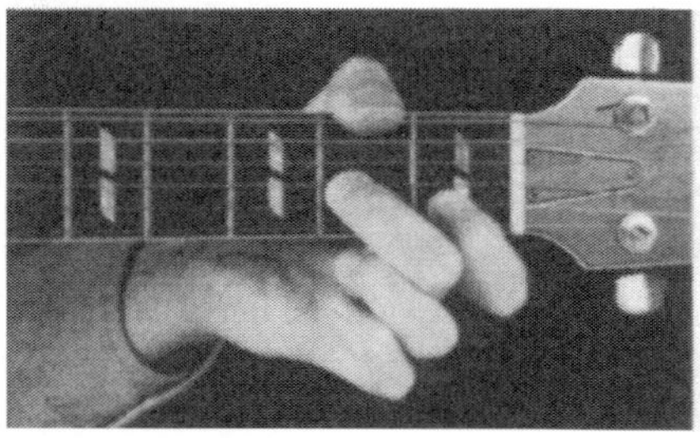

❼ **D7** chord

❽ **a♯** note

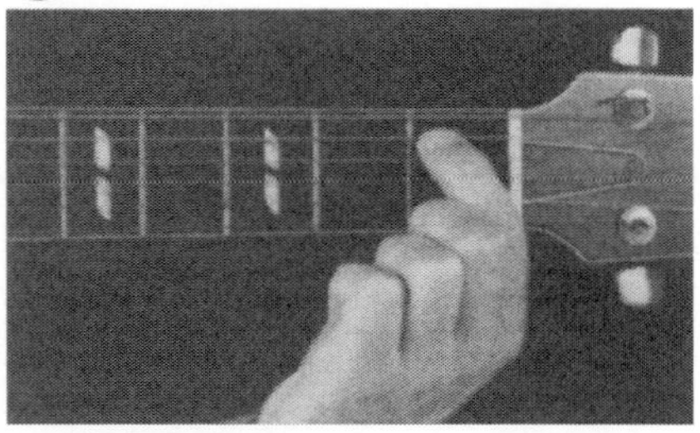

❾ **B7** chord

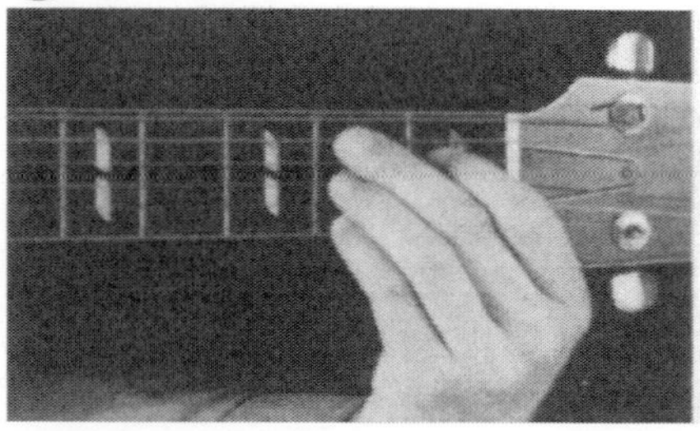

❿ **C** (with **high g**)

⓫ **c** note (with **a**)

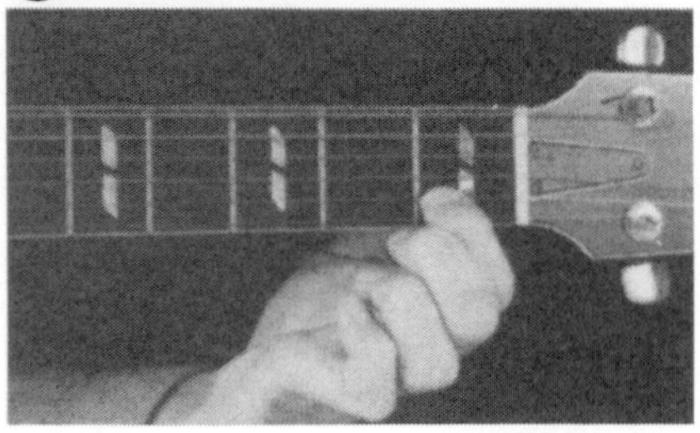

⓬ **b** and **d** notes

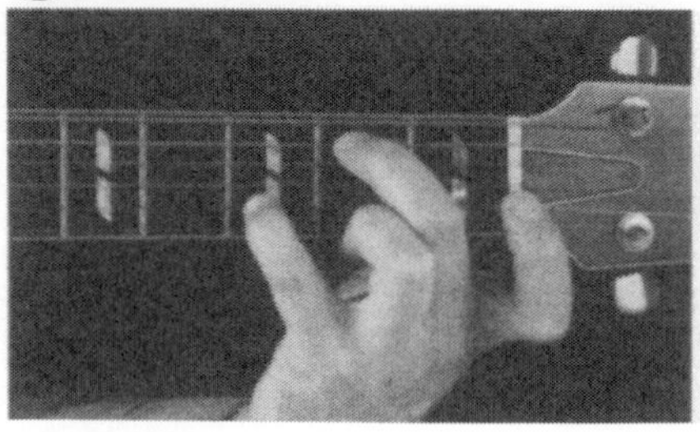

Imagine *Continued*

Verse

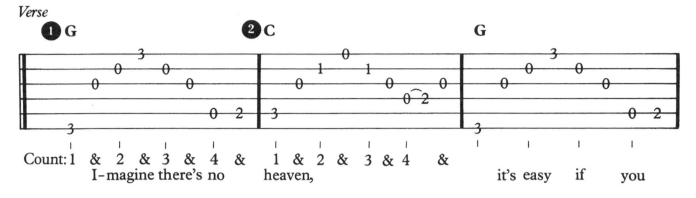

Count: 1 & 2 & 3 & 4 & 1 & 2 & 3 & 4 &

I-magine there's no   heaven,   it's easy   if   you

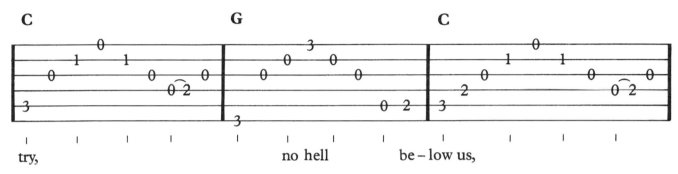

try,   no hell   be – low us,

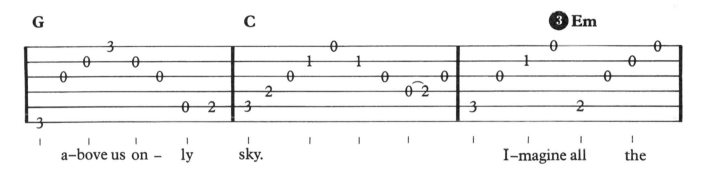

a–bove us on –   ly   sky.   I–magine all   the

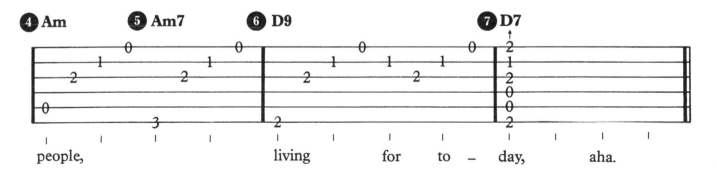

people,   living   for   to –   day,   aha.

Imagine Continued

Chorus

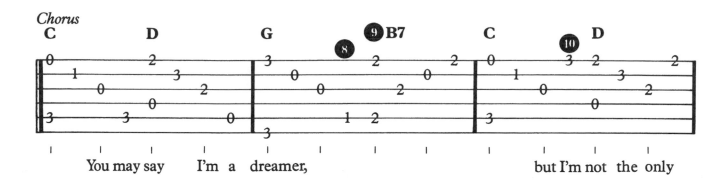

You may say   I'm a   dreamer,   but I'm not the only

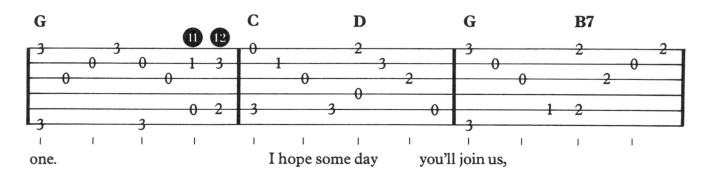

one.   I hope some day   you'll join us,

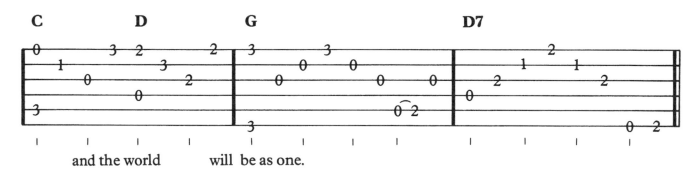

and the world   will be as one.

Verse 2:
Imagine there's no countries
It isn't hard to do
Nothing to kill or die for
And no religion too
Imagine all the people
Living life in peace, aha.

Verse 3:
Imagine no possessions
I wonder if you can
No need for greed or hunger
A brotherhood of man
Imagine all the people
Sharing all the world, aha.

Where Do You Go To My Lovely? Peter Sarstedt

Use either a flatpick or your right hand fingers held together to strum this song. I use a flatpick for strumming to save my nails for fingerpicking. It may take a while to be comfortable with the flatpick, but it's worth the effort.

Slight variations to the usual chord shapes are shown in the photos. They create more interest in this strumming style. Downstrums are used on the beats and upstrums between beats. The strum lengths are only approximate so don't try to be **too** precise with any of strumming accompaniments in this book.

The hammer-on notes should fall exactly half-way between beats. Where an upstrum comes before a chord change, open strings may often be struck – as in one **F** bar here. This keeps the rhythm going smoothly. The two fretted notes of the **Em** chord are hammered-on together in bar 16.

1 G chord

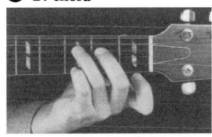

2 G7 chord

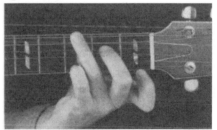

3 G6 chord

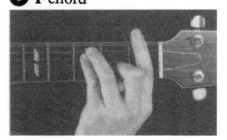

4 C chord

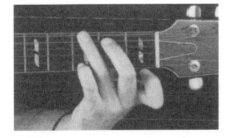

5 Em chord

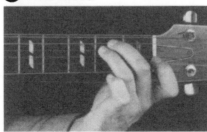

6 F chord

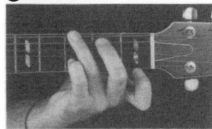

7 Dm chord

8 Dm7 chord

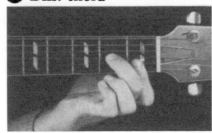

9 G6 chord

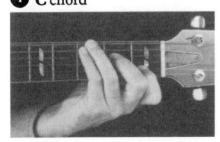

Where Do You Go To (My Lovely) Continued

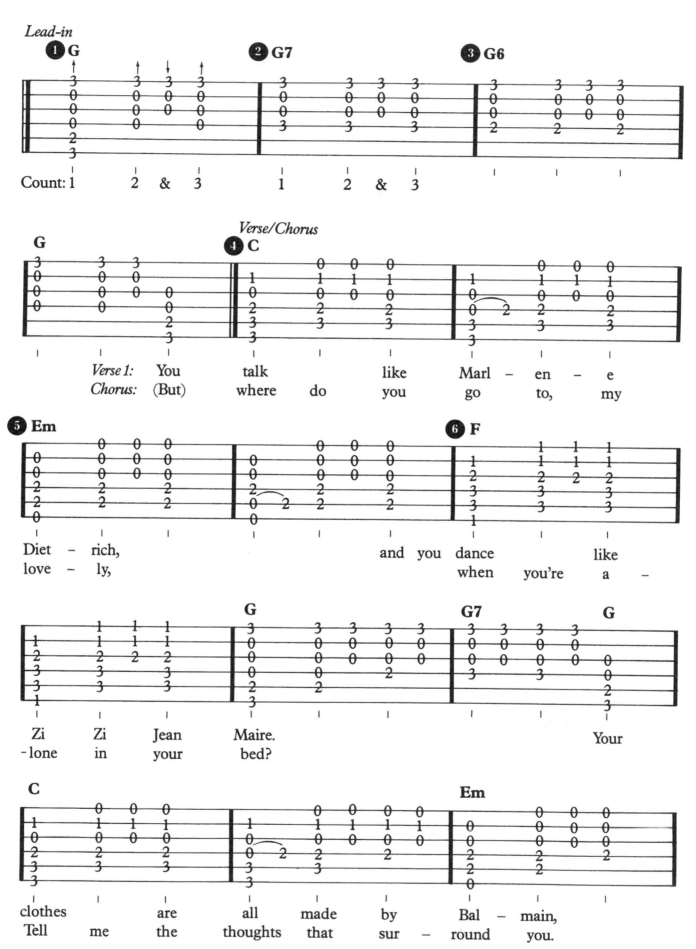

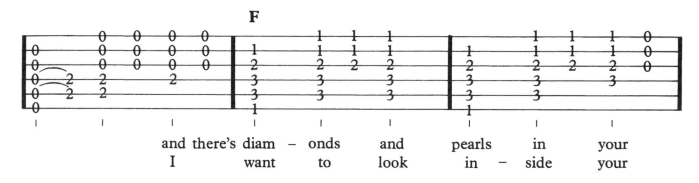

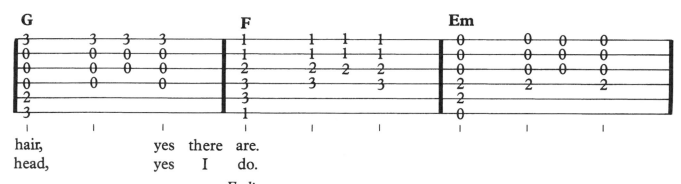

and there's diam – onds and pearls in your
I want to look in – side your

hair, yes there are.
head, yes I do.

Ending

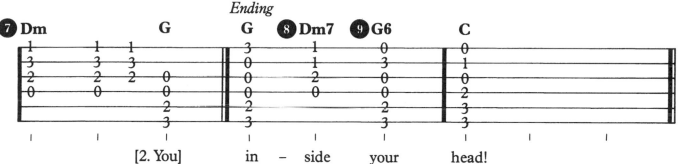

[2. You] in – side your head!

Verse 2:
You live in a fancy apartment
Off the Boulevard of St. Michelle
Where you keep your Rolling Stones records
And a friend of Sacha Distell, yes you do.

Verse 3:
I've seen all your qualifications
You got from the Sorbonne
And the painting you stole from Picasso
Your loveliness goes on and on, yes it does.

Verse 4:
When you go on your summer vacation
You go to Juan les Pins
With your carefully designed topless swimsuit
You get an even suntan, on your back and on your legs.

Verse 5:
And when the snow falls you're found in St. Moritz
With the others of the jet-set
And you sip your Napoleon brandy
But you never get your lips wet, no you don't.

Verse 6:
Your name it is heard in high places
You know the Aga Khan
He sent you a racehorse for Christmas
And you keep it just for fun, for a laugh, ha ha ha.

Verse 7:
They say that when you get married
It'll be to a millionaire
But they don't realise where you came from
And I wonder if they really care, or give a damn.

Verse 8:
I remember the back streets of Naples
Two children, begging in rags
Both touched with a burning ambition
To shake off their lowly born tags, they try.

Verse 9:
So look into my face, Marie-Claire
And remember just who you are
Now go and forget me forever
But I know you still bear the scar deep inside, yes you do.

Mountain Brush Russ Shipton

Like strumming accompaniments, the bass-strum style can be performed with a flatpick. To begin with it will be a little more difficult than using your thumb and fingers. You should try to produce a bouncy, country feel. This piece is straightforward and should be played fast eventually.

The 2nd and 4th left hand fingers should produce the **b** and **c♯** notes after the open **a** 5th string – this is a 'double hammer-on'.
Count it: 3 & 4.

① D chord

② A chord

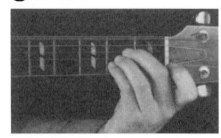

③ G chord

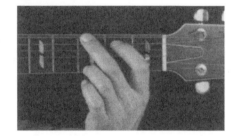

④ A7 chord

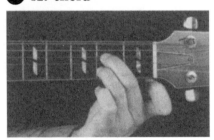

⑤ b note

⑥ c♯ note

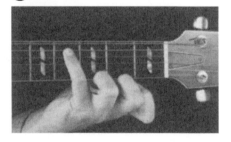

⑦ d♯ note

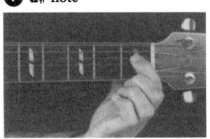

⑧ f♯ note

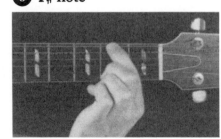

⑨ high d note

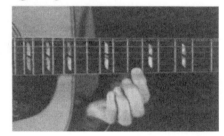

Mountain Brush Continued

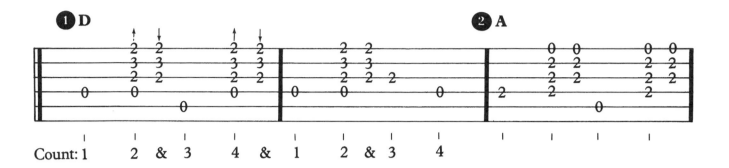

Count: 1 2 & 3 4 & 1 2 & 3 4

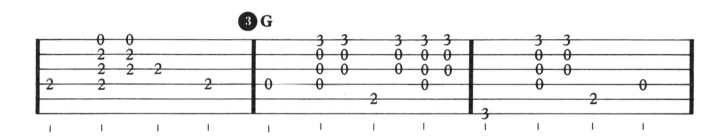

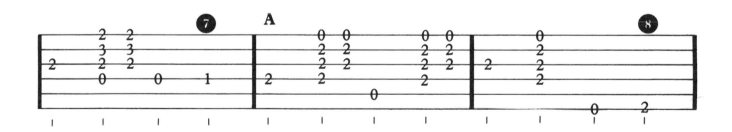

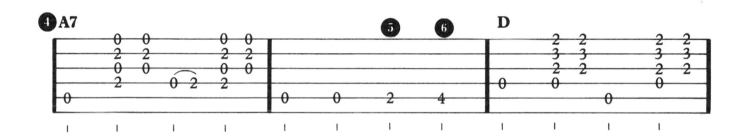

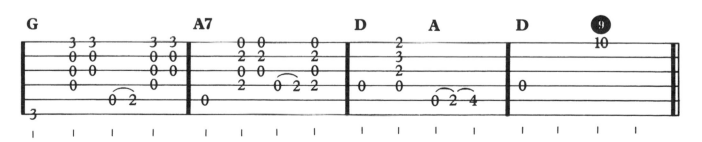

Lucille   Roger Bowling and Hal Bynum

Here is a similar, but longer piece with the bass-strum style. It has a waltz or 3/4 rhythm, however, and is in another key: A major.

The bass notes vary from chord to chord, and there are some hammer-ons and bass runs – all reasonably straightforward. The hammer-on in the **E** chord near the end of the first page is not 'within' the usual **E** shape, so you have to take your fingers off the chord to do these notes on the 6th string – use your 2nd and 4th fingers.

This accompaniment can be played 'straight' or with a slight swing in the rhythm – see page 3.

❶ A chord

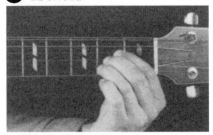

❷ E chord

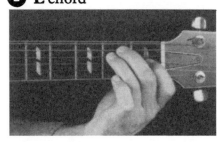

❸ Bm chord

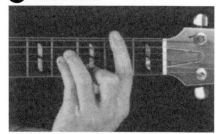

❹ f# note

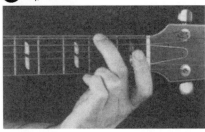

❺ g# note

❻ A7 chord

❼ D chord

❽ E7 chord

❾ c# note

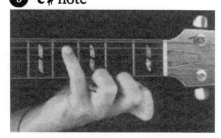

❿ b note

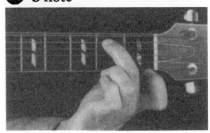

⓫ A add 9

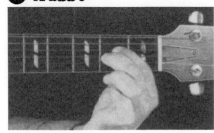

⓬ D add 9

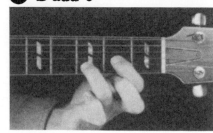

Lucille Continued

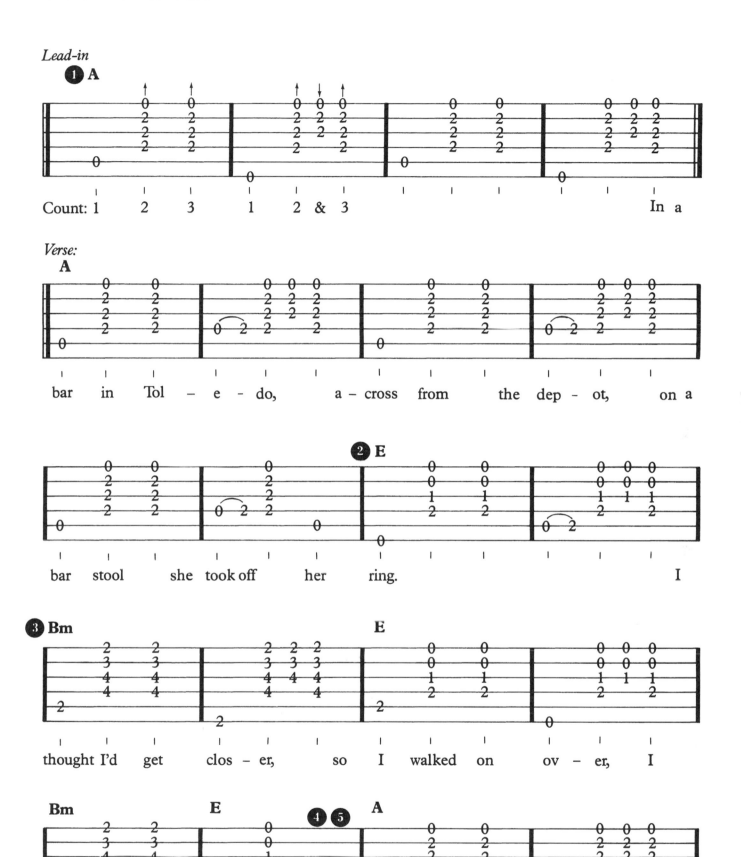

Lucille Continued

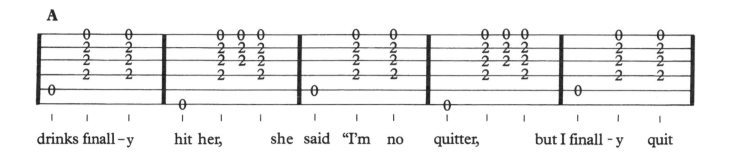

drinks finall – y   hit her,   she said "I'm   no   quitter,   but I finall – y   quit

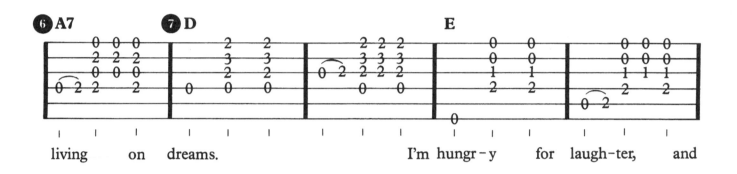

living   on   dreams.   I'm hungr – y   for   laugh-ter,   and

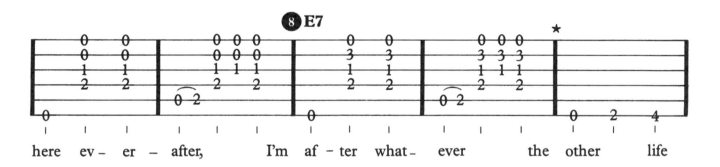

here   ev – er   –   after,   I'm af – ter   what – ever   the   other   life

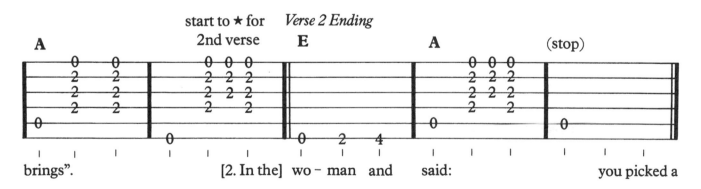

brings".   [2. In the] wo – man   and   said: you picked a

Chorus
[no guitar for 2 bars]

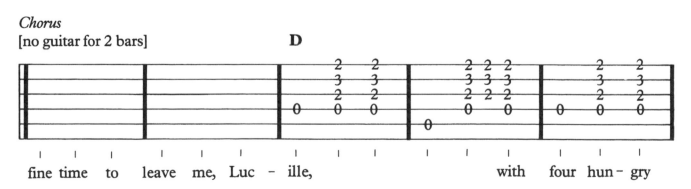

fine   time   to   leave   me,   Luc –   ille,   with   four   hun – gry

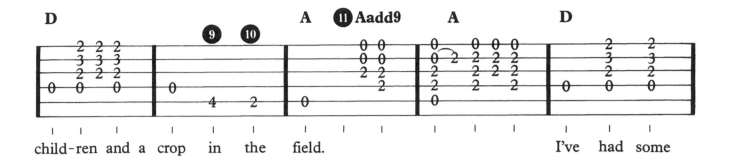

child-ren and a crop in the field. I've had some

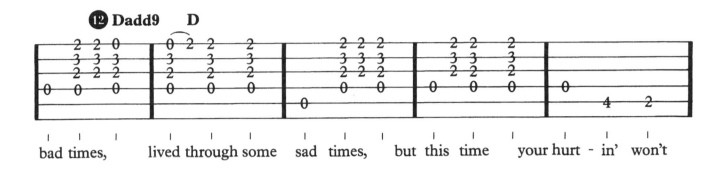

bad times, lived through some sad times, but this time your hurt - in' won't

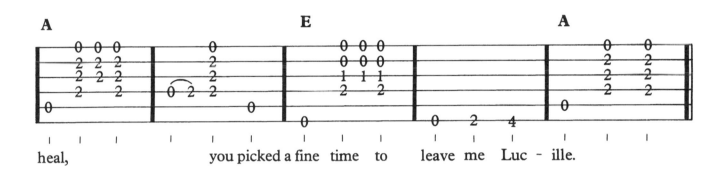

heal, you picked a fine time to leave me Luc - ille.

Verse 2:

In the mirror I saw him
And I closely watched him
I thought how he looked out of place.
He came to the woman
Who sat there beside me
He had a strange look on his face.
The big hands were calloused
He looked like a mountain
For a minute I thought I was dead.
But he started shaking
His big heart was breaking
He turned to the woman and said:

Verse 3:

After he left us
I ordered more whiskey
I thought how she made him look small.
From the lights of the bar-room
To a rented hotel room
We walked without talking at all.
She was a beauty
But when she came to me
She must've thought I'd lost my mind.
I couldn't hold her
'Cause the words that he told her
Kept coming back time after time:

Straight And Narrow   Russ Shipton

Here is an instrumental to warm you up for more difficult pieces in the alternating thumb style. Remember to play steady, evenly-spaced bass notes with your thumb. The treble notes can normally be played by your index and middle right hand fingers, though occasionally you can use your ring finger to make the rhythm flow smoother – for example, three fingers could be used in the penultimate bar which involves notes on all three treble strings.

The hammer-ons in this piece are all **on** to the beat, unlike those you've seen so far. The right hand strikes the string between beats and the left hand finger comes down on the beat at the **same** time as the thumb strikes the bass.

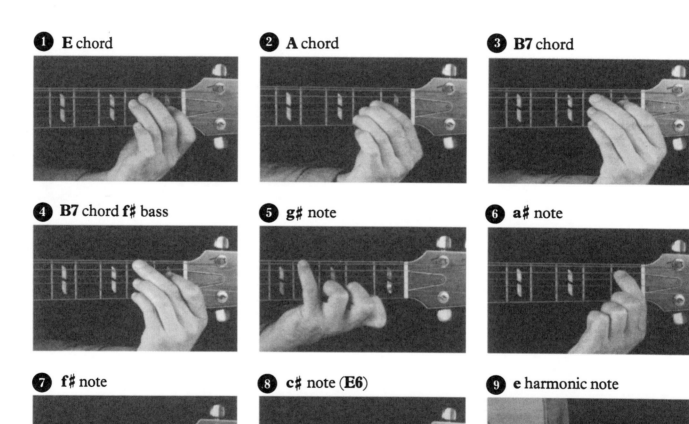

1. **E** chord
2. **A** chord
3. **B7** chord
4. **B7** chord **f♯** bass
5. **g♯** note
6. **a♯** note
7. **f♯** note
8. **c♯** note (**E6**)
9. **e** harmonic note

Straight And Narrow Continued

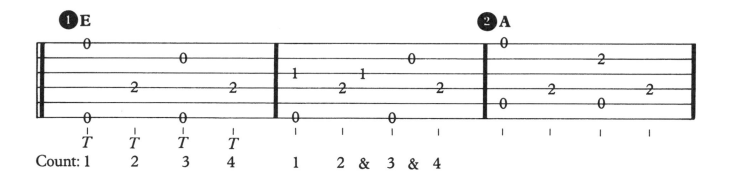

Count: 1   2   3   4   1   2 & 3 & 4

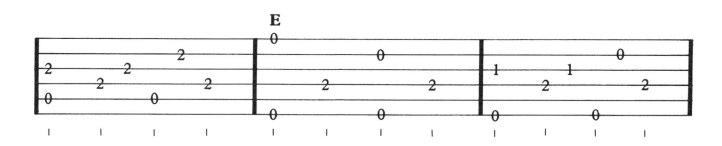

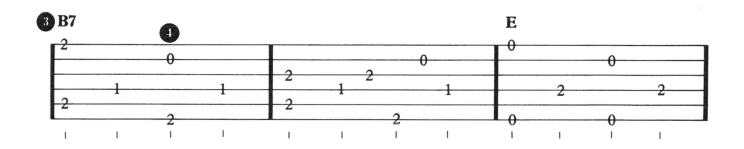

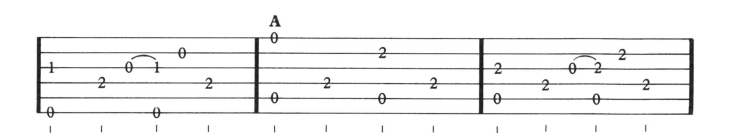

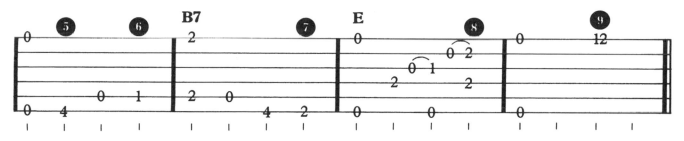

Last Thing On My Mind   Tom Paxton

Here's another alternating thumb arrangement – as played by Tom Paxton. The thumb strikes all the bass notes as in the previous piece, but **also** treble string notes if they're **on** the beat. i.e. in many bars of the lead-in and the **D** chord of the chorus.

The whole **D7** chord at the start of the 8th bar of the chorus can be placed on the strings as the hammer-on is performed.

Follow the tablature very carefully so you don't miss any of the bass changes and other notes that help to create an interesting accompaniment to complement the voice.

Count the first bar of the lead-in '3,4'.

1 **b** and **c** notes

2 **G** chord

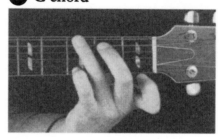

3 **C** chord

4 **D7** chord

5 **C** chord (**g** bass)

6 **D7** chord (**f♯** bass)

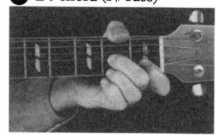

The Last Thing On My Mind Continued

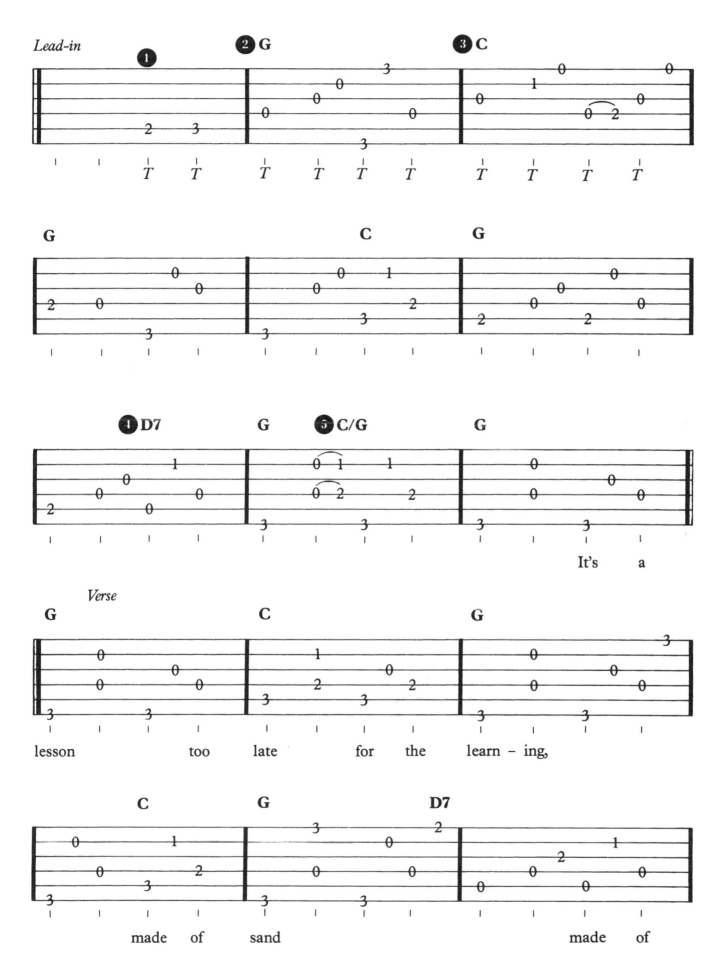

Lead-in

It's a

Verse

lesson   too   late   for   the   learn – ing,

made   of   sand   made   of

The Last Thing On My Mind   Continued

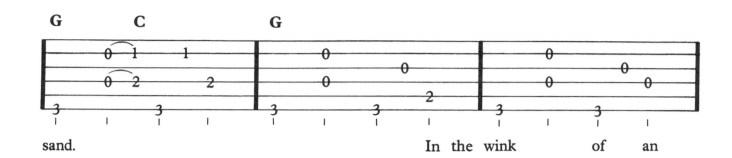

sand.   In the wink   of   an

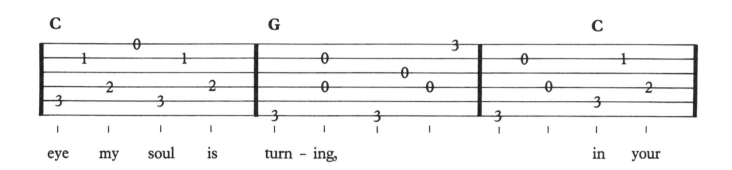

eye   my   soul   is   turn – ing,   in   your

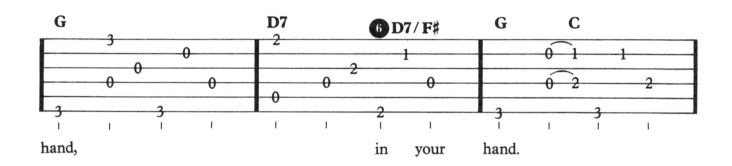

hand,   in   your   hand.

Chorus

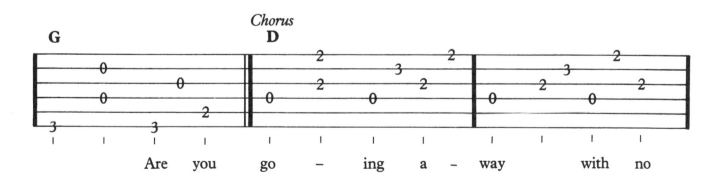

Are   you   go   –   ing   a   –   way   with   no

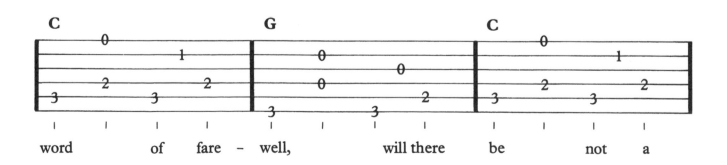

word   of   fare – well,   will there   be   not   a

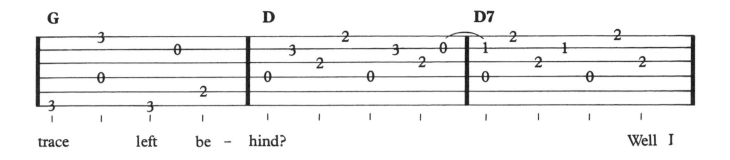

trace   left   be – hind?   Well   I

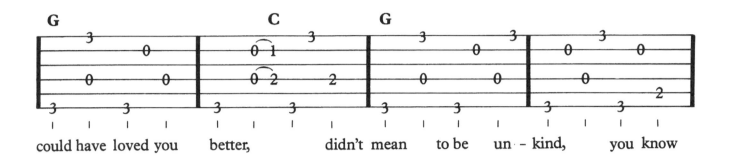

could have loved you   better,   didn't mean   to be   un – kind,   you know

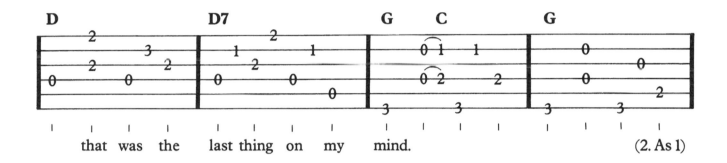

that was   the   last thing   on   my   mind.   (2. As 1)

Verse 2:
As I lie in my bed in the morning
Without you, without you
Each song in my breast dies a-borning
Without you, without you.

Verse 3:
You've got reason a-plenty for going
This I know, this I know
For the weeds have been steadily growing
Please don't go, please don't go.

Verse 4:
As I walk down the street the subway's rumbling
Underground, underground
While the thoughts in my head they're
a-jumbling
Round and round, round and round.

Sunny Bobby Hebb

Here's a classic song which sounds great with a driving, strumming accompaniment. It should be played fast with a lot of upstrums – you'll notice open strings before a chord change which I mentioned before an earlier piece. Make sure you get into position for the new chord on the next beat.

The **Fm** chord should be strummed and held till the final beat of the bar when it is strummed again.

Notice the length of the strums varies more – the upstrum between the 2nd and 3rd beats is emphasised, and the 3rd beat has a shorter strum on the bass strings only.

The penultimate bar involves a 'double-time' strum on the final beat – a thin flatpick would help to get these smoother. Experiment with double-strumming as it helps to break up a simple strumming accompaniment and add more interest.

(Strum indications are given just for the 1st bar, but remember that the whole piece must be strummed).

❶ Am chord

❷ C chord

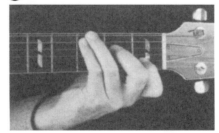

❸ F chord

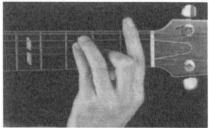

❹ E chord

❺ E7 chord

❻ Am7 chord

❼ F maj7 chord

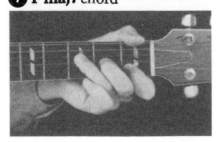

❽ Fm chord

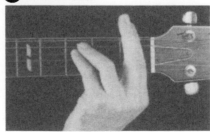

Sunny Continued

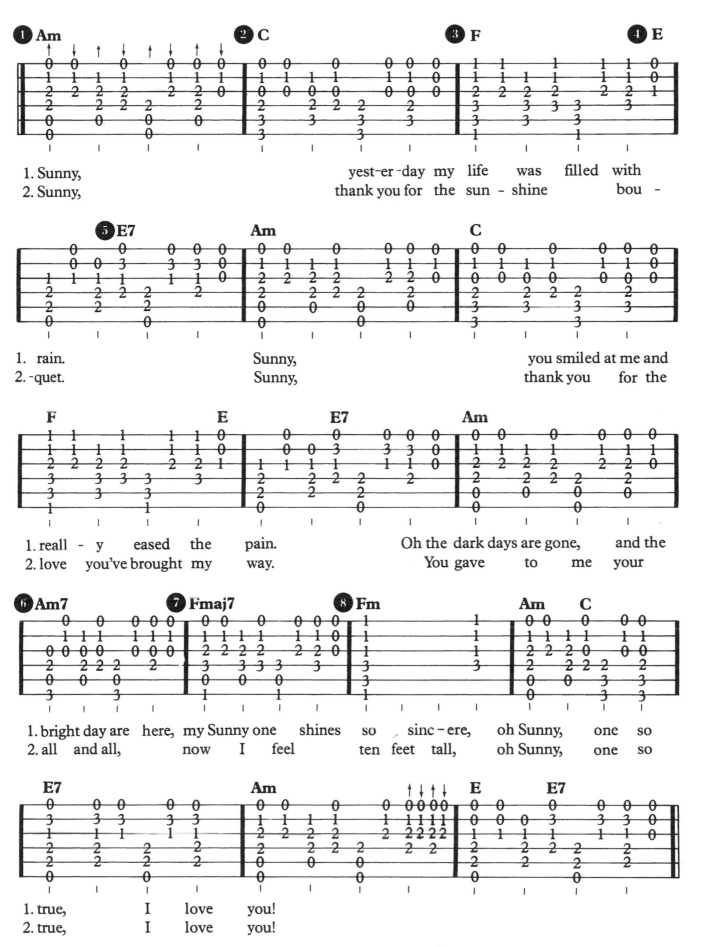

1. Sunny,   yest-er-day my life   was   filled with
2. Sunny,   thank you for the sun - shine   bou -

1. rain.   Sunny,   you smiled at me and
2. -quet.   Sunny,   thank you   for the

1. reall - y   eased   the   pain.   Oh the dark days are gone,   and the
2. love   you've brought my   way.   You gave   to   me   your

1. bright day are here, my Sunny one   shines   so   sinc - ere,   oh Sunny,   one so
2. all   and all,   now   I feel   ten feet tall,   oh Sunny,   one so

1. true,   I   love   you!
2. true,   I   love   you!

No Woman, No Cry Vincent Ford

This accompaniment looks easier than it is. The tablature is written with 4 beats in each bar, but there should be more stress on the 1st and 3rd beats. The song is a ballad, but the beats as shown are played reasonably quickly.

The strums are often quite short – try to approximate what is shown, but the strum length can vary a little provided you're holding the chord shapes as shown in the photographs.

Notice the **F** chord coming in 'early' on the 4th beat of the 3rd bar of verse and chorus. Hold this **F** chord over the 1st beat of the next bar.

The run in the 6th bar could be played with single notes – the **f, e, d** and **c** bass notes of the chords shown. Hold the **C** chord over the 1st beat of the following bar.

❶ C chord

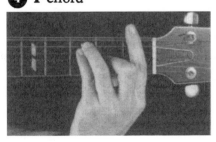

❷ G6 chord (**b** bass **add c**)

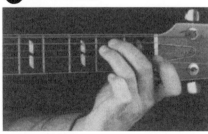

❸ Am chord

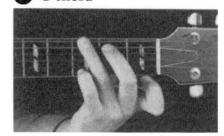

❹ F chord

❺ Em chord

❻ G chord

No Woman, No Cry Continued

Chorus

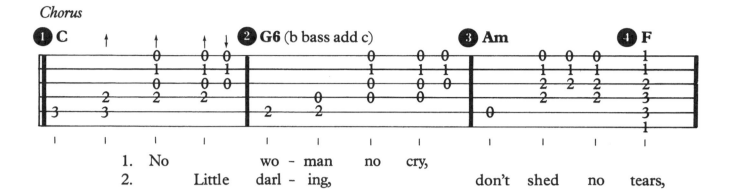

1. No   wo - man   no   cry,
2. Little darl - ing,   don't shed   no   tears,

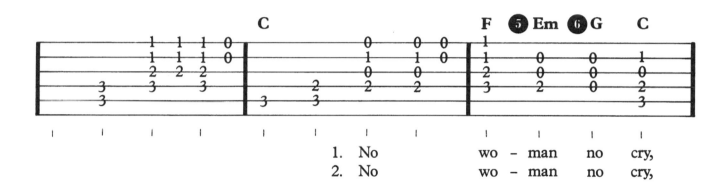

1. No   wo - man   no   cry,
2. No   wo - man   no   cry,

[*Rpt.* 8 bars] *Verse* (Play these 4 bars eight times)

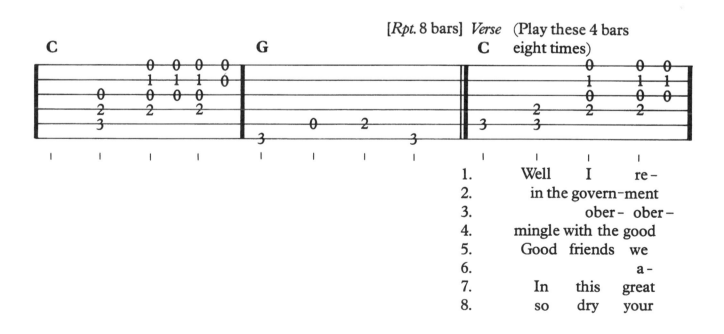

1.   Well   I   re -
2.   in the govern-ment
3.   ober - ober –
4.   mingle with the good
5.   Good friends we
6.   a -
7.   In   this great
8.   so   dry   your

No Woman, No Cry Continued

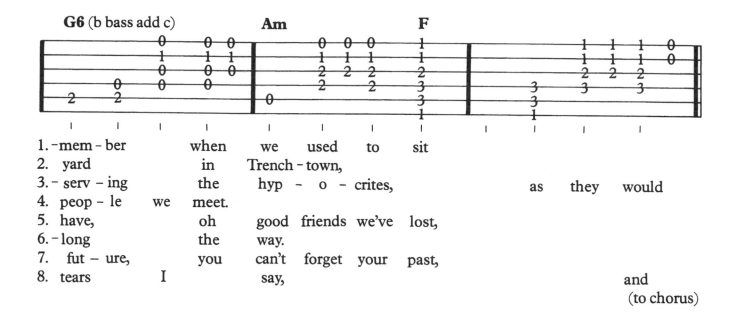

1. -mem - ber		when	we	used	to	sit		
2. yard		in	Trench - town,					
3. - serv – ing		the	hyp – o – crites,				as	they would
4. peop – le	we	meet.						
5. have,		oh	good	friends	we've	lost,		
6. -long		the	way.					
7. fut – ure,		you	can't	forget	your	past,		
8. tears	I		say,				and	

(to chorus)

Middle Section

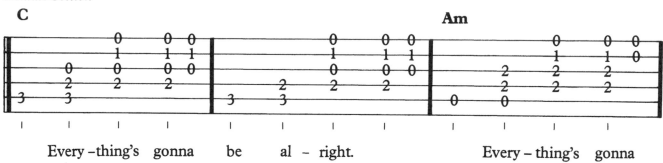

Every –thing's gonna be al – right.   Every – thing's gonna

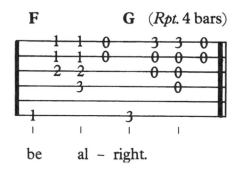

be al – right.

Verse 2:
Well I remember when we used to sit
In the government yard in Trenchtown
And then Georgie would make the firelight
As it was logwood burning through the night
Then we would cook cornmeal porridge
Of which I'll share with you
My feet is my only carriage
So I've got to push on through.

Everybody's Talkin' Fred Neil

This arrangement involves the alternating thumb style with straightforward chords, apart from the **D** and **D maj7** chords which are fingered with a half barré. Use the standard D chord for the middle section.

Again we have hammer-ons **onto** the beat, so make sure your left hand finger and right hand thumb produce notes at exactly the same time.

Remember that the right hand thumb plays **all** the notes on the beat in the alternating thumb style unless otherwise indicated.

The alternating thumb patterns in this accompaniment include many treble notes between beats – this gives the appropriate rolling, flowing effect for this kind of song.

This accompaniment should be played at a medium pace.

❶ D chord

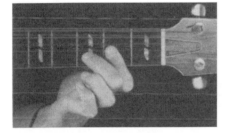

❷ Dmaj7 chord

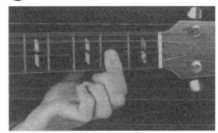

❸ D7 chord

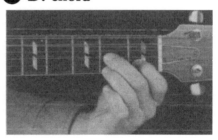

❹ Em chord

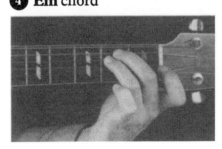

❺ A7 chord

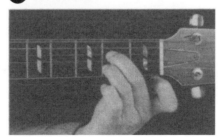

Everybody's Talkin' Continued

Verse

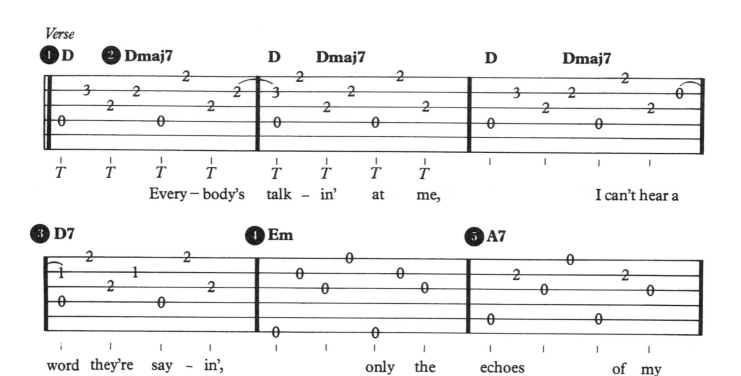

Every – body's   talk – in'   at   me,   I can't hear a

word   they're   say – in',   only   the   echoes   of   my

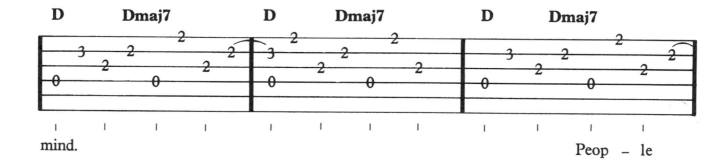

mind.   Peop – le

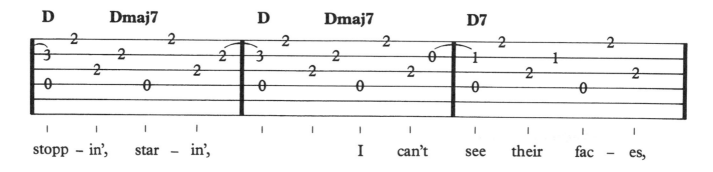

stopp – in',   star – in',   I   can't   see   their   fac – es,

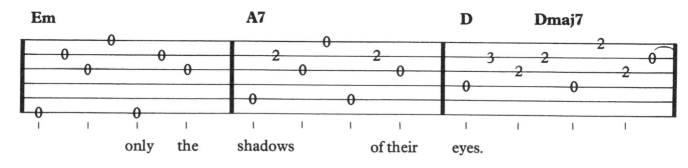

only   the   shadows   of their   eyes.

Middle Section

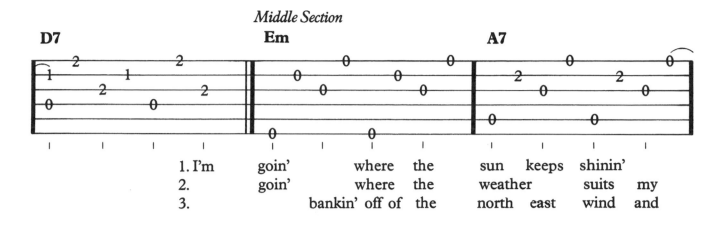

1. I'm goin' where the sun keeps shinin'
2. goin' where the weather suits my
3. bankin' off of the north east wind and

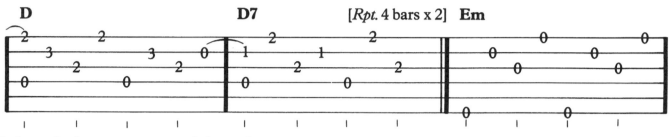

1. through the pourin' rain,
2. clo – o – othes,
3. sailin' on summer breeze, and skippin' over the

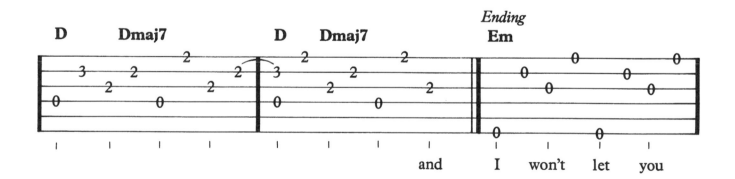

ocean like a stone.

Ending

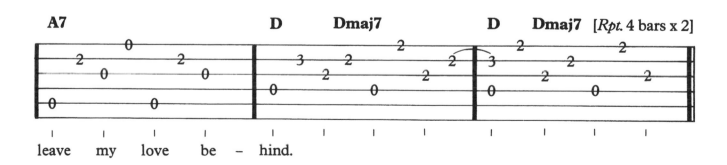

and I won't let you

leave my love be – hind.

Catch The Wind Donovan

This is a very close transcription of Donovan's accompaniment. He is very adept at the bass-strum style and uses a flatpick to produce both a full and smooth sound.

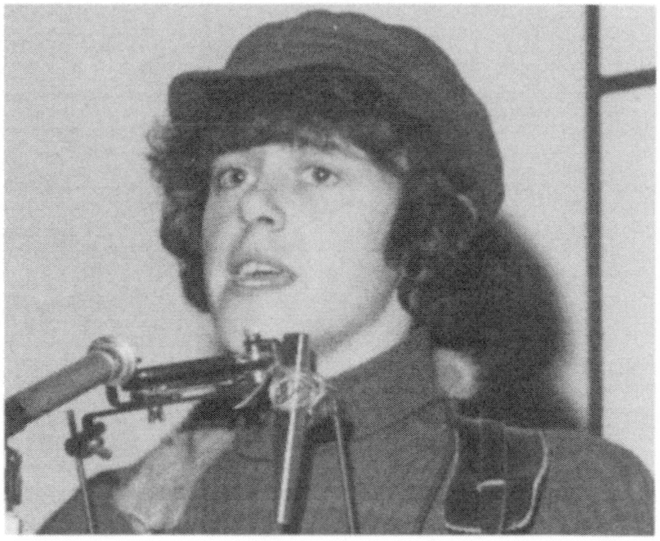

You'll notice that the first three chord shapes involve the little finger on the **g** note of the 1st string. Leaving this note ringing throughout the changes makes the harmonies interesting as well as making the finger moves easier.

Watch the bass runs carefully. They are often part of the melody and need to stand out above the strums. Make the strums quite short and not too heavy.

❶ **C** chord

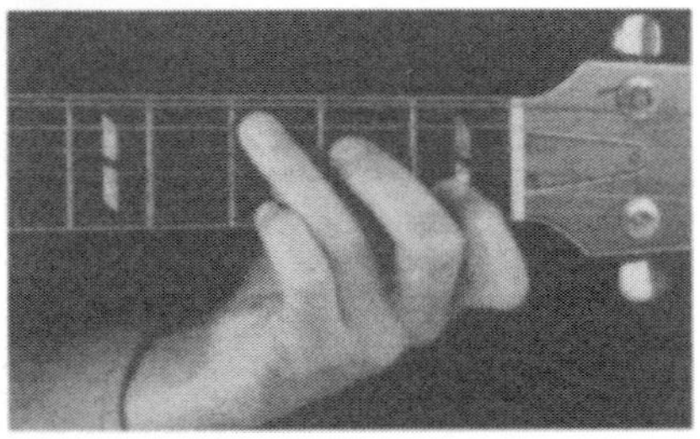

❷ **F add 9** chord

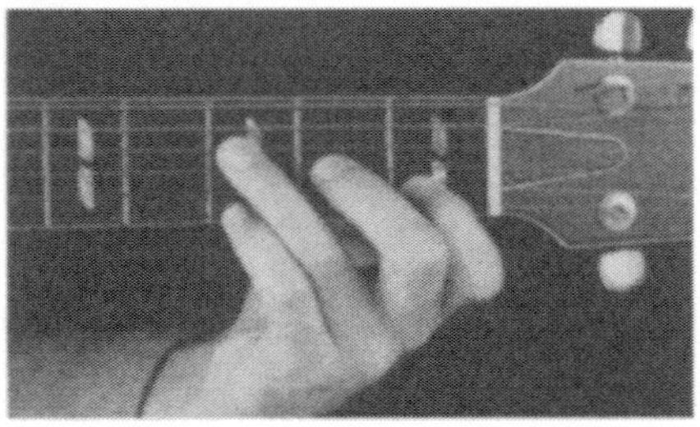

❸ **G** chord

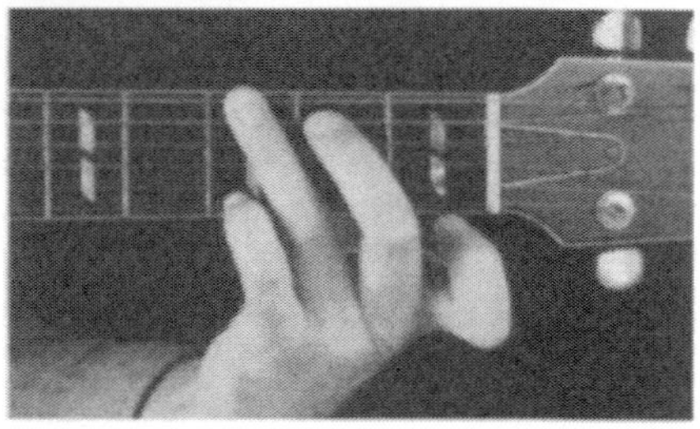

❹ **F** chord

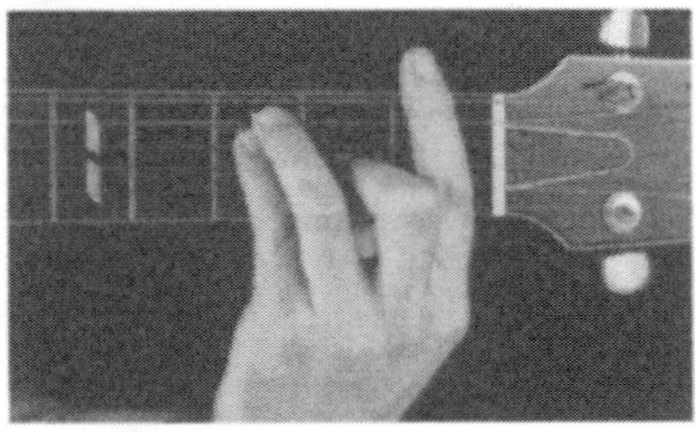

❺ **Gsus** chord

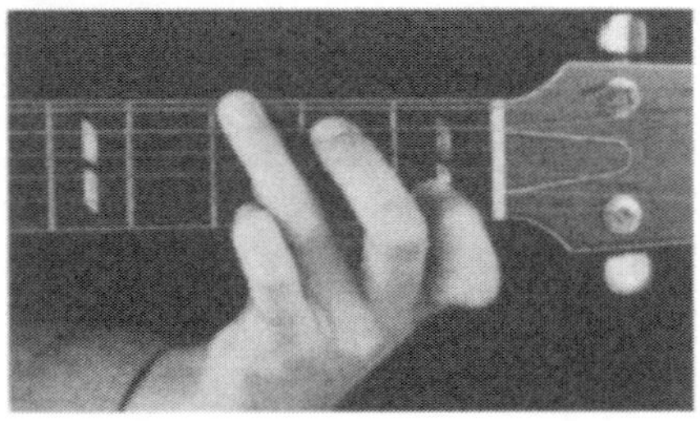

❻ **Em** chord

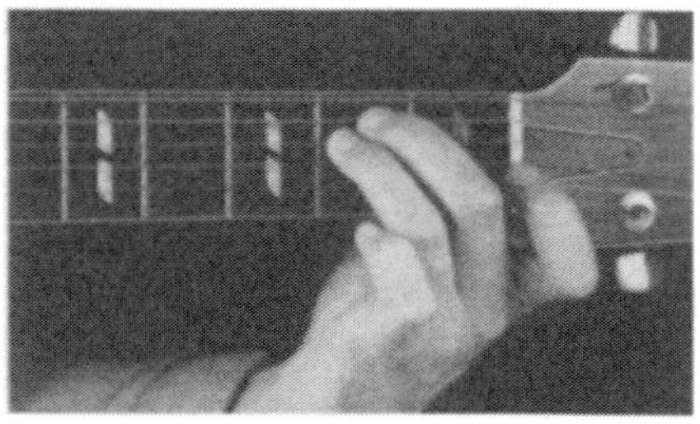

❼ **D7** chord

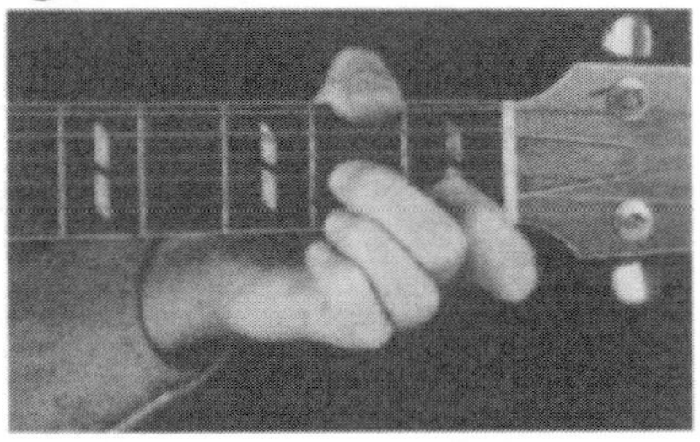

❽ **G6** chord

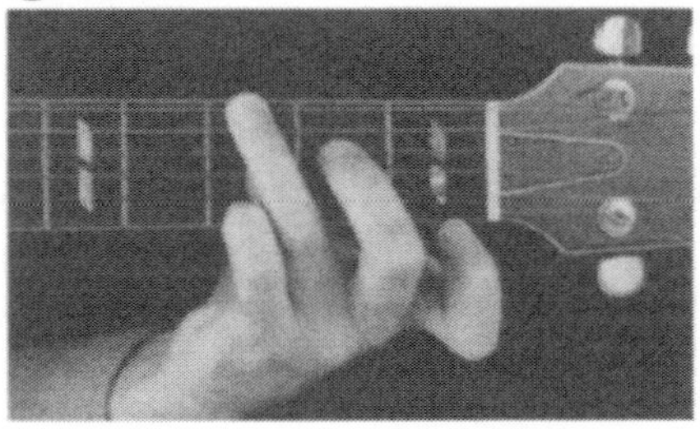

❾ **G7** chord

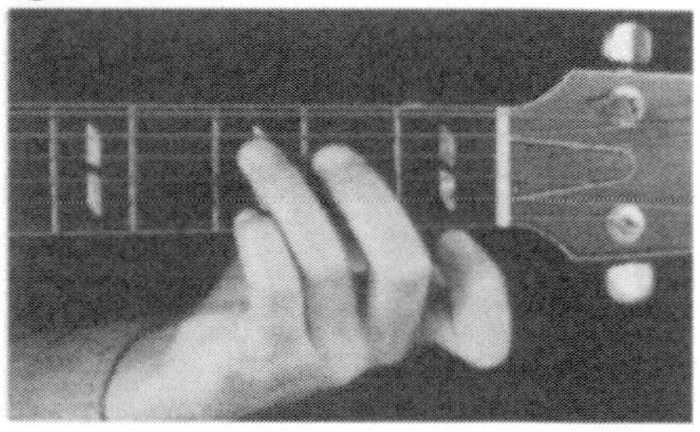

Catch The Wind Continued

Level 2 (right margin, vertical)

Lead-in

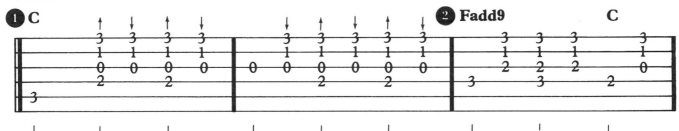

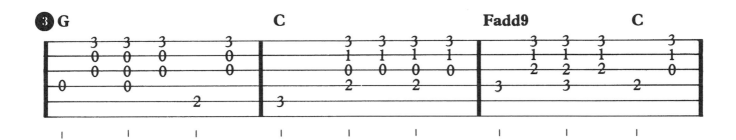

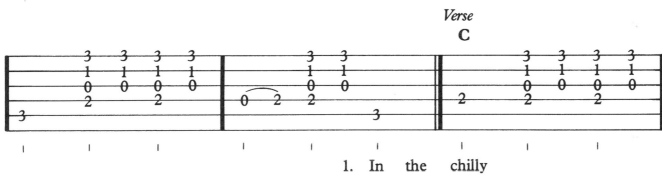

1. In the chilly
2. feel you

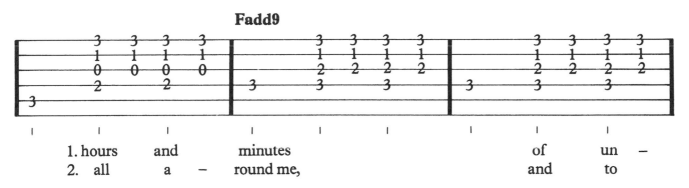

1. hours   and   minutes   of   un –
2. all   a – round me,   and   to

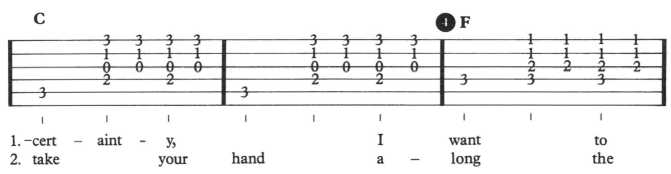

1. –cert – aint – y,   I   want   to
2. take   your   hand   a – long   the

Catch The Wind Continued

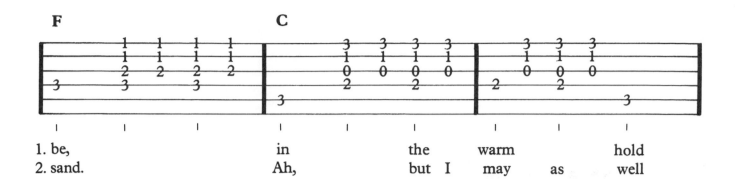

1. be,		in	the	warm	hold
2. sand.		Ah,	but I	may	as	well

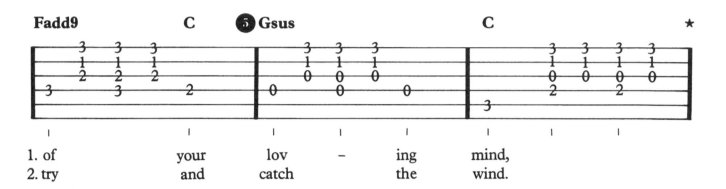

1. of		your	lov	–	ing	mind,
2. try		and	catch		the	wind.

[Rpt. 1st 13 Bars
of Verse to ★]

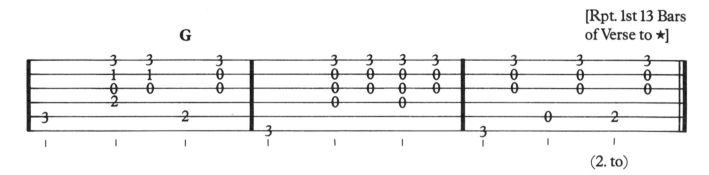

(2. to)

[To Verse 2]

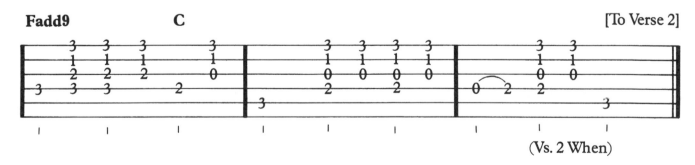

(Vs. 2 When)

Middle Section

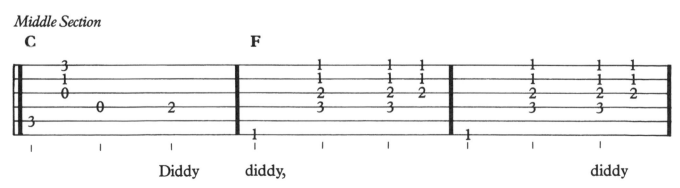

		Diddy	diddy,	diddy

32

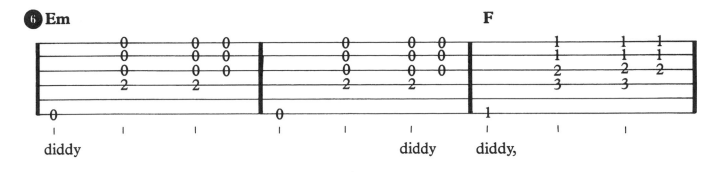

diddy   diddy   diddy,

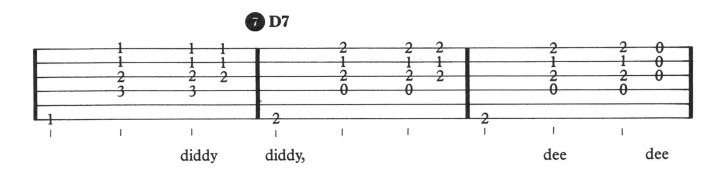

diddy   diddy,   dee   dee

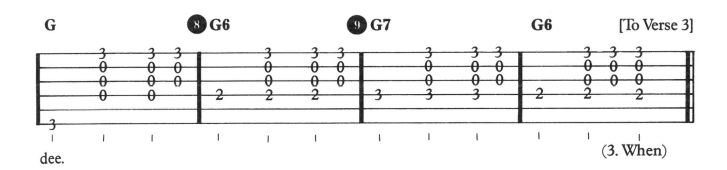

dee.   (3. When)

Verse 2:
When sundown pales the sky
I want to hide a while behind your smile
And everywhere I'd look your eyes I'd find
For me to love you now
Would be the sweetest thing, 'twould make me
sing
Ah, but I may as well try and catch the wind.

Verse 3:
When rain has hung the leaves with tears
I want you near to kill my fears
To help me to leave all my blues behind
Standin' in your heart
Is where I want to be and long to be
Ah, but I may as well try and catch the wind.

Canadian Hornpipe Russ Shipton

This is another alternating thumb piece, but with a distinct difference – the rhythm is swung. All styles and patterns can be made to 'swing' by delaying the strums or notes that come between beats. When these notes between beats are played for the more usual 'straight' rhythm, they are placed exactly halfway between the beats. But for a swing rhythm you need to delay playing them until just before the following beat. The longer you delay, the stronger the swing feeling will be.

The basic chord positions for this piece are straightforward, but fingers are put on and taken off frequently and quickly. To build up speed will take time. Take each bar slowly to start with, making sure you spot all the runs and changes.

The hammer-on and pull-off on the top string (in the 5th, 6th and 8th bars) should be performed very quickly. In fact, in the space of half a beat, or to be precise, just under half a beat, to take account of the swing. The three notes would be three equal semiquavers (triplet) in musical terms.

Follow the photos carefully for the fingering – some changes are a bit tricky. Add your little finger for the **g** note in the first two bars, and add your 3rd and 4th fingers for the **d**, **f♯**, and **g** notes in the 3rd bar.

The right hand thumb plays all notes on the beat, except where they are treble notes. These, as in bars 2 and 4, should be played by the index and middle fingers on the right hand. Try to alternate these two fingers when playing notes one after the other on the same string – this will make the rhythm smoother.

This piece should be played quite fast.

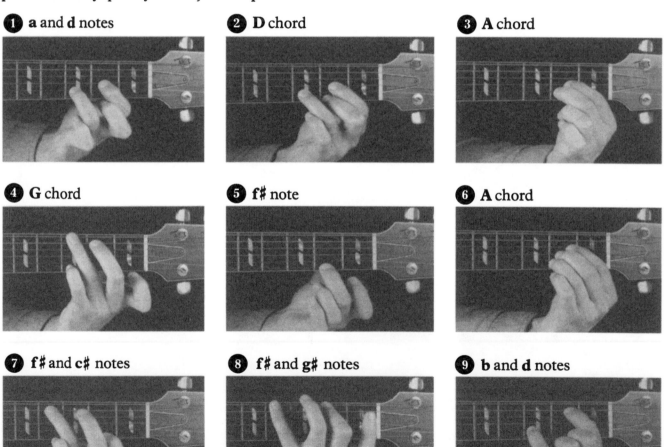

① **a** and **d** notes   ② **D** chord   ③ **A** chord

④ **G** chord   ⑤ **f♯** note   ⑥ **A** chord

⑦ **f♯** and **c♯** notes   ⑧ **f♯** and **g♯** notes   ⑨ **b** and **d** notes

Canadian Hornpipe Continued

Level 2

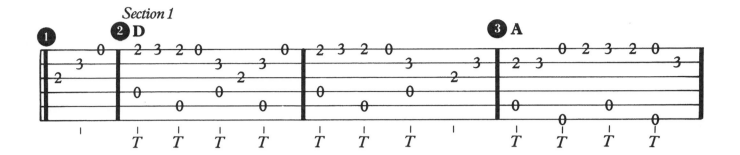

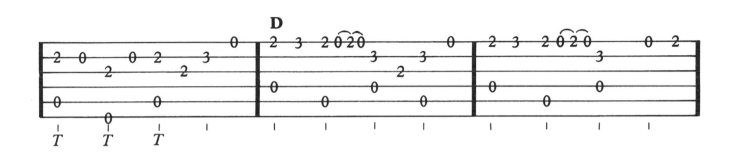

[Rpt. Section 1]

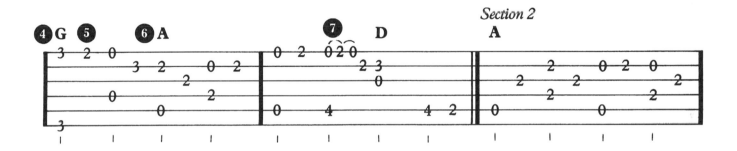

35

Streets Of London Ralph McTell

Ralph McTell has always played this great song with the same chords and using the alternating thumb style, but he's made numerous small changes to the accompaniment over the years. I've included a number of these changes here. Watch out for all the little things that make the arrangement interesting.

Not all the chord positions have been shown in the photos – the **C, Am, F** and **Em** chords are all the usual shapes, except where indicated.

The 1st and 4th fingers can be added to the 3rd finger **G** chord (shown in the last photo) for the run on the 2nd string in the 7th bar of the chorus. Add your little finger to the usual **C** chord (on the 3rd fret of the 4th string) to produce the **C sus** chord for the ending. Then strum across the **C** chord to finish.

Remember that the right hand thumb plays all of the beat notes in this type of accompaniment. The index and middle fingers of the right hand are normally sufficient for alternating thumb pieces of medium tempo like this, but where all three treble strings are involved you could use your ring finger for the treble notes as well.

1 **G chord** (**b** bass)

2 **Em7** chord

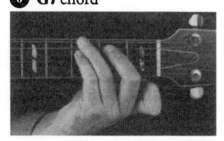

3 **C chord** (**g** bass)

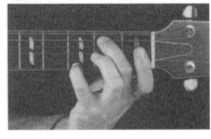

4 **F6** chord

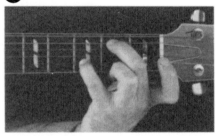

5 **G7 add 6** chord

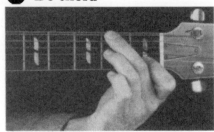

6 **G7** chord

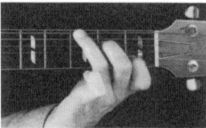

7 **Am7** chord

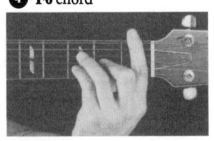

8 **D9** chord

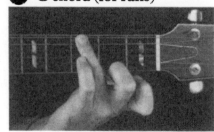

9 **G** chord (for runs)

Streets Of London Continued

Verse

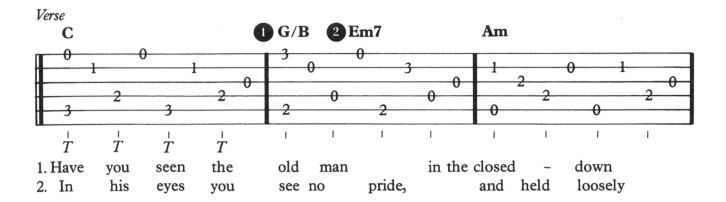

1. Have you seen the old man in the closed – down
2. In his eyes you see no pride, and held loosely

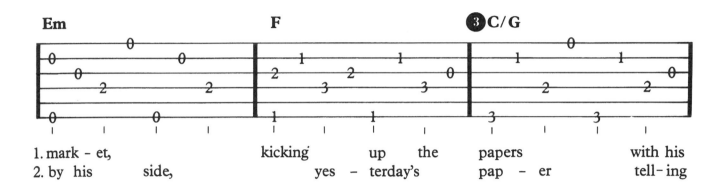

1. mark - et, kicking up the papers with his
2. by his side, yes – terday's pap – er tell- ing

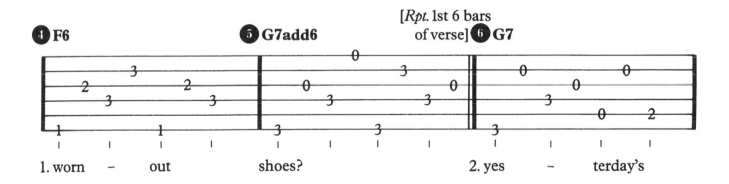

1. worn – out shoes? 2. yes – terday's

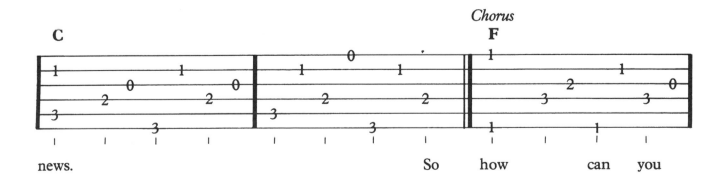

news. So how can you

Streets Of London Continued

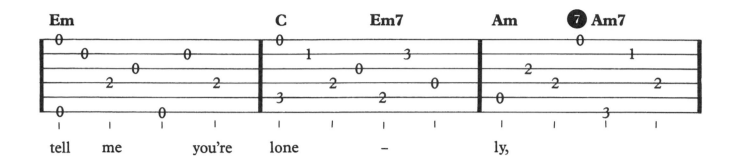

tell   me   you're   lone   –   ly,

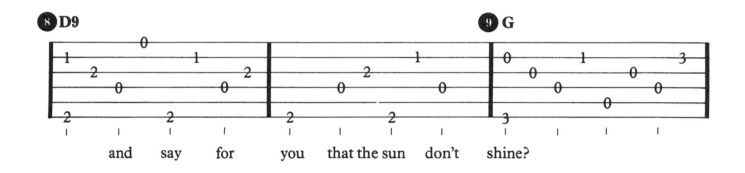

and   say   for   you   that the sun   don't   shine?

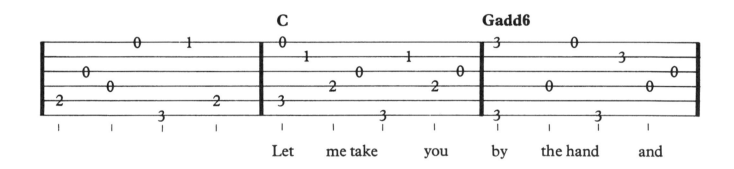

Let   me take   you   by   the hand   and

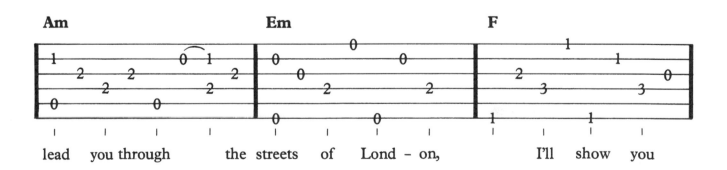

lead   you through   the streets   of   Lond – on,   I'll   show   you

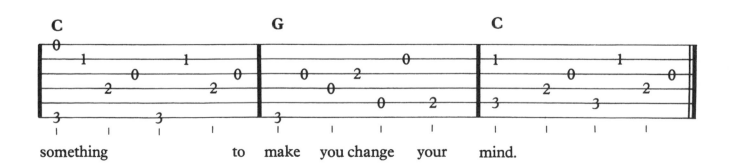

something   to   make   you change   your   mind.

Tag

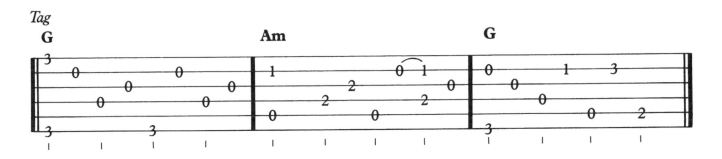

Ending

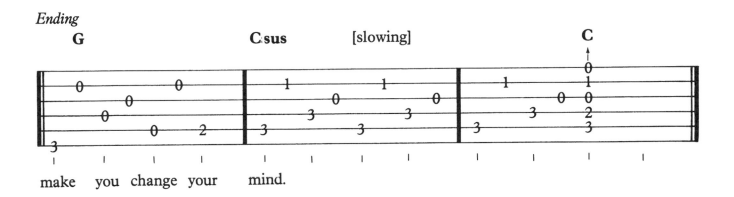

make you change your   mind.

Verse 2:
Have you seen the old gal who walks the streets
of London
Dirt in her hair and her clothes in rags?
She's no time for talking, she just keeps right on
walking
Carrying her home in two carrier bags.

Verse 3:
And in the all-night café, at a quarter-past eleven
Same old man sitting there on his own
Looking at the world over the rim of his tea-cup
Each tea lasts an hour, then he wanders home
alone.

Verse 4:
And have you seen the old man outside the
seaman's mission
His memory fading with those medal ribbons
that he wears
And in our winter city, the rain cries a little pity
For one more forgotten hero, and a world that
doesn't care.

Scarborough Fair Paul Simon

Here's Paul Simon's great arrangement for this beautiful old song. Don't worry too much about the fancy names for some of the chords – they're actually easy to finger!

Use the right hand thumb on the beat notes except where indicated. Make sure you stress the beat notes in the first two bars to produce a clear 3/4 rhythm. With two thumb strikes off the beat, you might end up with 6/8 or 123, 123 effect, which won't be right.

The chords are all shown in the photos and are straightforward. The bass run from **Am** to **C** is very common – raise the 2nd finger from the 4th to 5th string.

The 1st and 2nd fingers on the **C** chord in the 1st bar of the 2nd page are pulled-off together. Pull the strings a little before letting go, to produce clear open string notes.

❶ Am7sus 4 (add 6) chord

❷ Am (add 9) chord

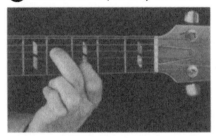

❸ G chord

❹ C chord (g bass)

❺ C chord

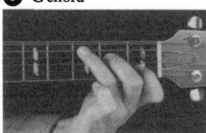

❻ D chord

❼ Am chord

❽ b and d notes

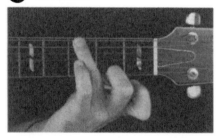

❾ c note

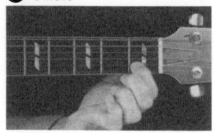

Scarborough Fair Continued

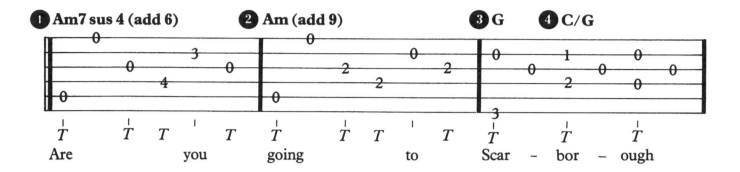

1 Am7 sus 4 (add 6) **2** Am (add 9) **3** G **4** C/G

Are   you   going   to   Scar - bor - ough

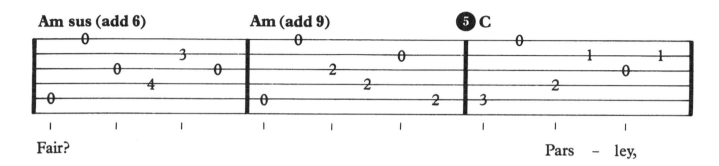

Am sus (add 6) Am (add 9) **5** C

Fair?   Pars - ley,

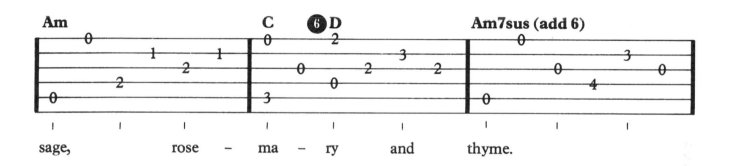

Am C **6** D Am7sus (add 6)

sage,   rose - ma - ry   and   thyme.

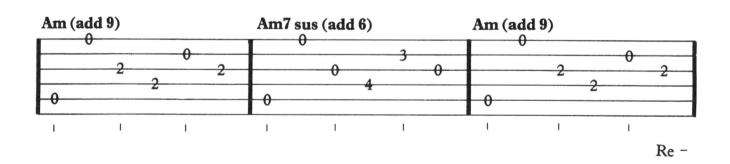

Am (add 9) Am7 sus (add 6) Am (add 9)

Re -

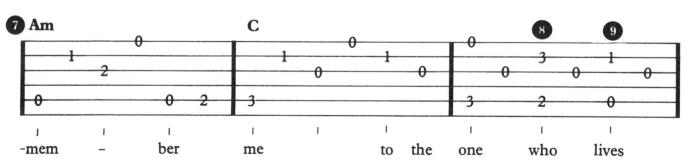

7 Am C **8** **9**

-mem - ber   me   to   the   one   who   lives

Scarborough Fair Continued

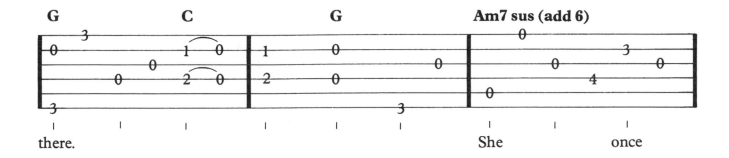

there.   She   once

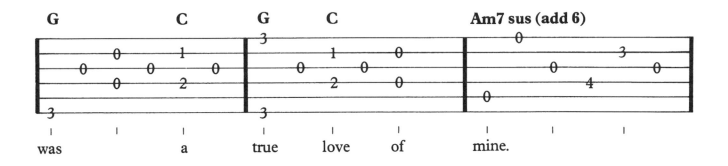

was   a   true   love   of   mine.

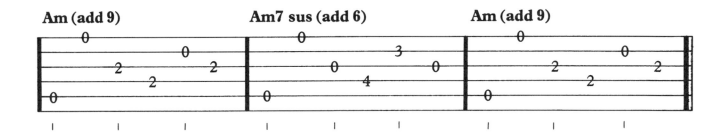

Verse 2:
Tell her to make me a cambric shirt
Parsley, sage, rosemary and thyme
Without no seams, nor needlework
Then she'll be a true love of mine.
Verse 3:
Tell her to find me an acre of land
Parsley, sage, rosemary and thyme
Between the salt water and the sea strands
Then she'll be a true love of mine.
Verse 4:
Tell her to reap it with a sickle of leather
Parsley, sage, rosemary and thyme
And gather it all in a bunch of heather
Then she'll be a true love of mine.

Your Song Elton John & Bernie Taupin

The main right hand pattern for this Elton John classic is a cross between the alternating thumb style and what may be called the 'syncopated arpeggio style'. The right hand thumb strikes twice at the start of the pattern, on the 1st beat and on the half beat immediately after. Then it plays the bass notes on the 3rd and 4th beats. You can still count most bars quite simply: 1 & 2 & 3 & 4 &; in musical terms, 8 quavers.

Once you get used to this new kind of pattern you should find the chord shapes and runs straightforward, except perhaps the **f** to **f♯** to **g** run near the end of the verse. If you bar the

F chord right across with your 1st finger, you should raise the 2nd finger for the **f♯** on the 6th string without moving the bar until the open 3rd string is played at the end of the bar.

As you can see from the photo, the **F6** chord involves the left hand thumb fingering the 6th string **f** note – it's good to be flexible and use thumb or finger where necessary.

Note that the **G11** is virtually the same as an **F** chord with a **g** bass – leave your fingers in the **F** position and move your 3rd finger to the 6th string.

❶ C chord (**g** bass)

❷ Fmaj7 chord

❸ G chord (**f♯** bass)

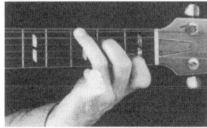

❹ Am7 chord

❺ D9 chord

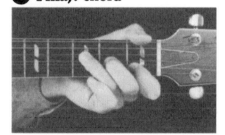

❻ E7 chord

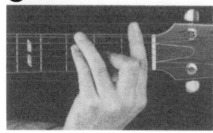

❼ b note

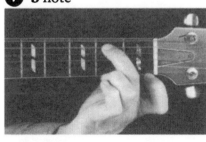

❽ Dm chord

❾ G sus 4 chord

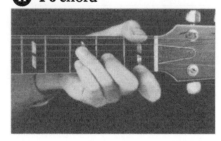

❿ C sus 4 chord (**g** bass)

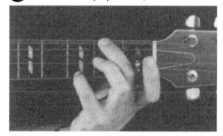

⓫ F6 chord

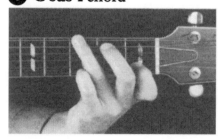

⓬ G11 chord

43

Your Song Continued

Level 2

Verse

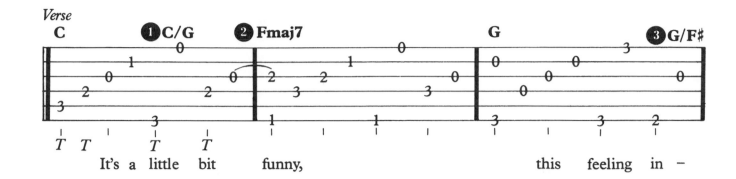

It's a little bit funny, this feeling in –

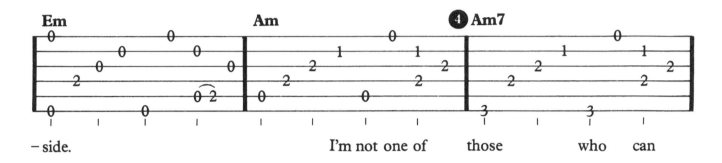

– side. I'm not one of those who can

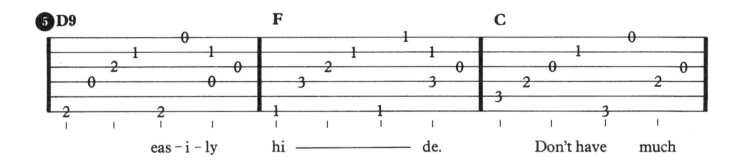

eas‑i‑ly hi ——————— de. Don't have much

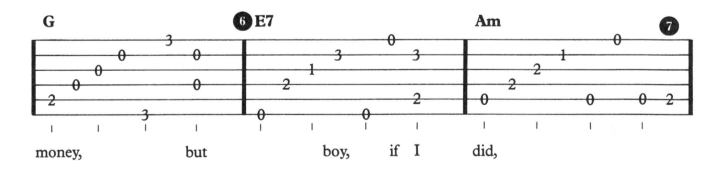

money, but boy, if I did,

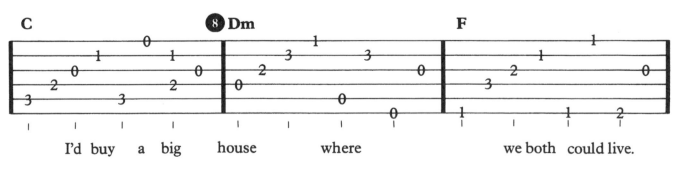

I'd buy a big house where we both could live.

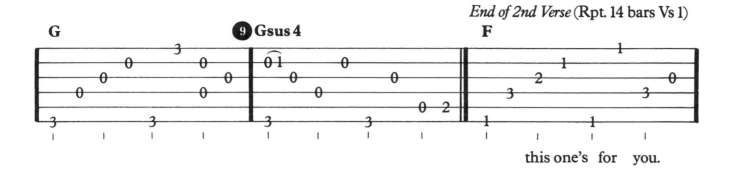

G   ❾ **Gsus 4**   *End of 2nd Verse* (Rpt. 14 bars Vs 1) **F**

this one's for   you.

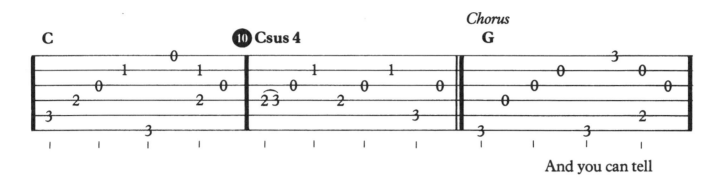

C   ❿ **Csus 4**   *Chorus* **G**

And you can tell

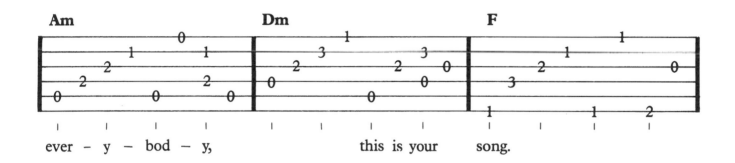

Am   **Dm**   **F**

ever – y – bod – y,   this is your   song.

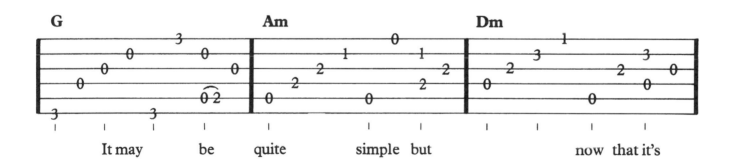

G   **Am**   **Dm**

It may   be   quite   simple but   now that it's

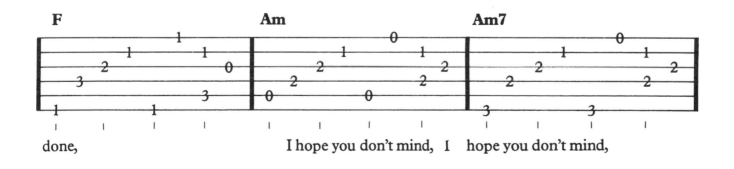

F   **Am**   **Am7**

done,   I hope you don't mind, I hope you don't mind,

Your Song Continued

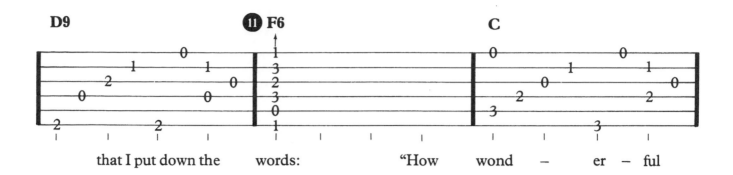

that I put down the words: "How wond — er — ful

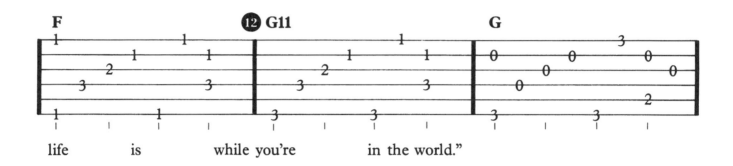

life is while you're in the world."

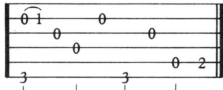

Verse 2:
If I was a sculptor, but then again, no
Or a man who makes potions in a travelling show
I know it's not much but it's the best I can do
My gift is my song, and this one's for you.

Verse 3:
I sat on a roof, and kicked off the moss
Well a few of the verses, they got me quite cross
But the sun's been quite kind while I wrote this song
It's for people like you that keep me turned on.

Verse 4:
So excuse me forgetting, but these things I do
You can see I've forgotten if they're green or they're blue
Anyway, the thing is, what I really mean
Yours are the sweetest eyes I've ever seen.

I'll Have To Say I Love You In A Song Jim Croce

This beautiful ballad will help to strengthen your bar chords. The arrangement follows Jim Croce's playing very closely, and he uses what I call the syncopated arpeggio style. The right hand thumb plays between the 2nd and 3rd beats. It may help you to count each bar: 123, 123, 12, though in musical terms it's still a simple bar of 8 quavers.

Notice the open string note before some chord changes to make them easier. These notes are struck lightly.

The **E** chord bass run to the **Amaj7** is a stretch for the left hand, but not too difficult. These runs help to make the accompaniment more interesting, as do the hammer-ons. These should be played quickly, as in the last piece. The open string is struck on the halfbeat, so the two notes last just half a beat together – in musical terms they are two semiquavers.

1 **Amaj7** chord
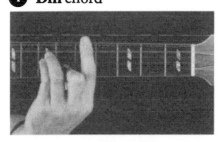

2 **C#m** chord
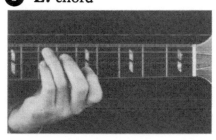

3 **Bm** chord
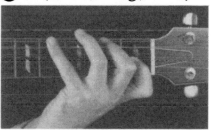

4 **Dm** chord

5 **E7** chord
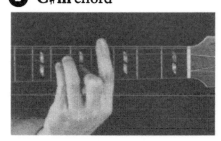

6 **E** (then **f#** and **g#** notes)
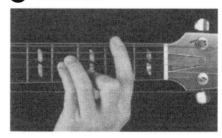

7 **E** (then **b** and **c#** notes)
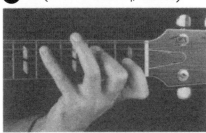

8 **D** chord

9 **D#°** chord
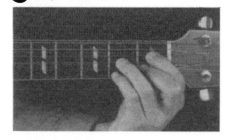

10 **C#7** chord
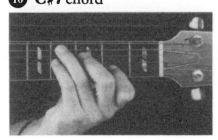

11 **F#m** chord
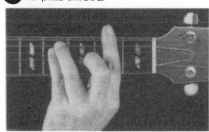

12 **A** chord

I'll Have To Say I Love You In A Song Continued

Introduction

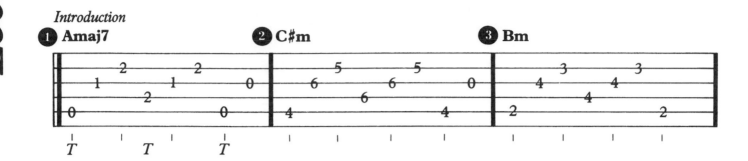

❶ **Amaj7**　　　　❷ **C#m**　　　　❸ **Bm**

Verse

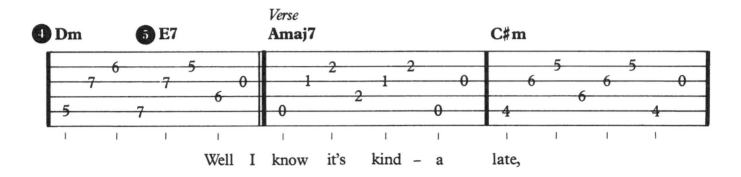

❹ **Dm**　❺ **E7**　**Amaj7**　　　　**C#m**

Well I know it's kind – a late,

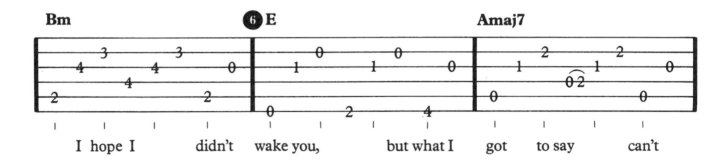

Bm　　　　❻ **E**　　　　**Amaj7**

I hope I didn't wake you, but what I got to say can't

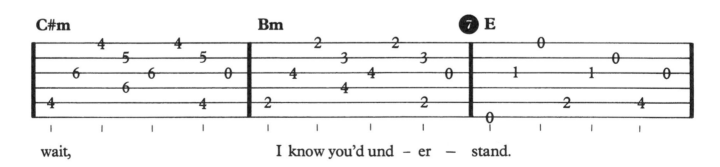

C#m　　　　**Bm**　　　　❼ **E**

wait, I know you'd und – er – stand.

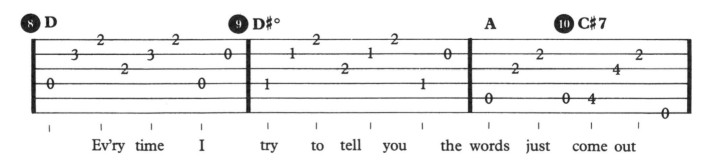

❽ **D**　　　❾ **D#°**　　　**A**　❿ **C#7**

Ev'ry time I try to tell you the words just come out

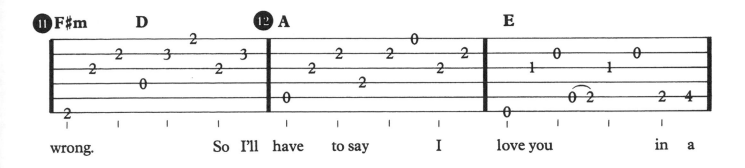

wrong.   So I'll have   to say   I   love you   in a

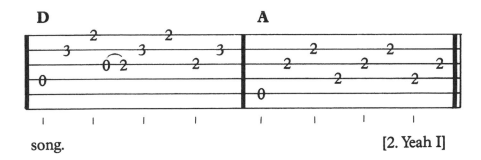

song.   [2. Yeah I]

Verse 2:
Yeah I know it's kind of strange
But every time I'm near you
I just run out of things to say
I know you'd understand
Every time I tried to tell you
The words just came out wrong
So I'll have to say I love you in a song.

Verse 3:
(Instrumental)
Every time the time was right
All the words just came out wrong
So I'll have to say I love you in a song.

Verse 4:
Yeah I know it's kind of late
I hope I didn't wake you
But there's something that I just got to say
I know you'd understand
Every time I tried to tell you
The words just came out wrong
So I'll have to say I love you in a song.

Huskie Trot Russ Shipton

This arrangement includes some unusual chords. The little finger comes on for the **c** note in the **Eaug** chord. Leave the other fingers down as you do this. Similarly, leave the other two fingers on when you move the 3rd finger for the **g♯** note on the bass string for the **C♯7** chord. Then leave the 1st finger down when the 2nd finger comes over for the **g** note on the 6th string.

The little finger moves along the 1st string to the 3rd fret for the ♯**5** (**g**) note of the **B7** chord. Then it moves back to its original position. The 2nd finger moves from the 5th to the 6th string. The 1st and 3rd fingers remain where they are. The **d** note of the **E7** chord (played at the end of **E** bar) should ring on throughout the next bar.

The 3rd finger on the **A** chord stays where it is while the 1st and 2nd fingers move to produce the **A7**(♭**9**) chord.

The right hand thumb plays all the beat notes in this alternating thumb piece. The tempo should be moderate.

1 **E aug** chord

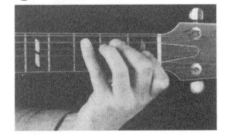

2 **C♯7 (add ♭3)** chord

3 **F♯6** chord

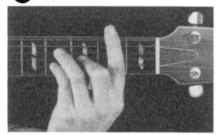

4 **F♯7** chord

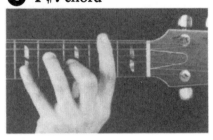

5 **C♯m** chord

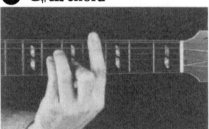

6 **B7♯5** chord

7 **B7** chord (**f♯** bass)

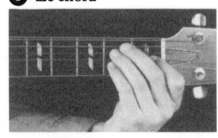

8 **E6** chord

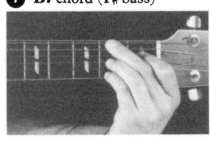

9 **f♯** note

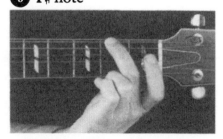

10 **g♯** note

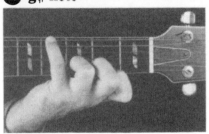

11 **E7** chord

12 **A7** (♭**9** bass) chord

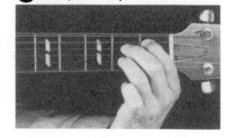

Huskie Trot Continued

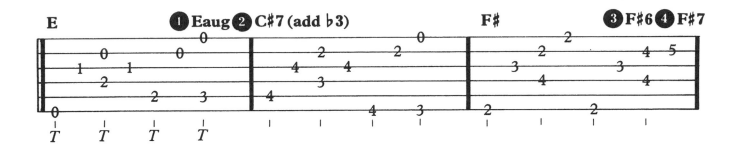

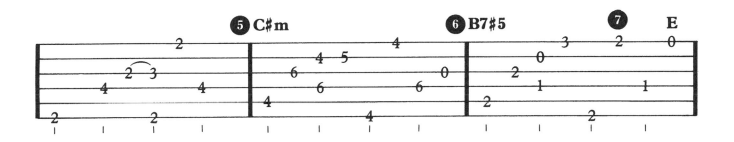

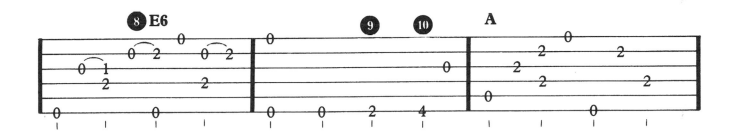

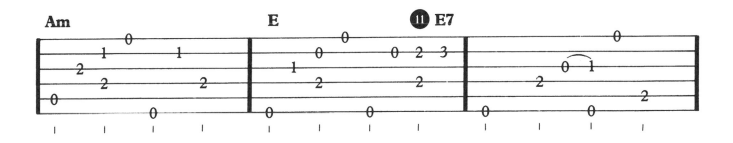

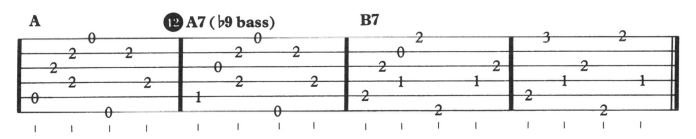

Only You   Vincent Clarke

This song was a hit with a heavy, electronic arrangement, and then an even bigger hit when sung a cappella. It works successfully on acoustic guitar as well, using a similar mixed style as we did for 'Your Song'. There are variations to the opening pattern, though. The 2nd bar for example, is normal alternating thumb, and some bars in the chorus have two thumb strikes off the beat. They're all counted 1 & 2 & 3 & 4 &, but produce slightly different rhythmic effects.

Notice the 'wow' on the **d** note (the 9th of the **C9** chord). Push the string slightly upwards and then release pressure on the string to damp the sound in this case.

The melody is picked out in the break, while the bass notes of the basic chords are played. Move your 1st and 4th fingers for the melody notes, and keep your 2nd and 3rd fingers in the usual places for the **C** and **G** chords.

The pull-off in the 1st bar of the break is done with the 1st finger, and the open 1st string note comes exactly halfway between beats. The end hammer-on is played quickly.

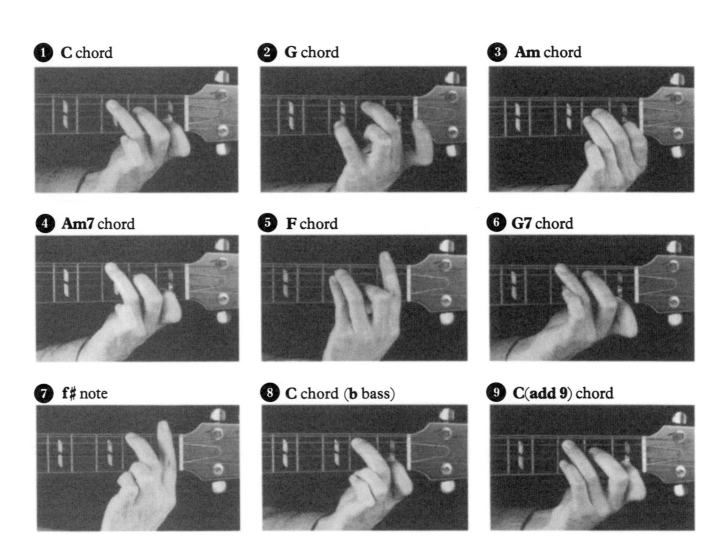

1 **C** chord

2 **G** chord

3 **Am** chord

4 **Am7** chord

5 **F** chord

6 **G7** chord

7 **f♯** note

8 **C** chord (**b** bass)

9 **C(add 9)** chord

Only You Continued

Verse

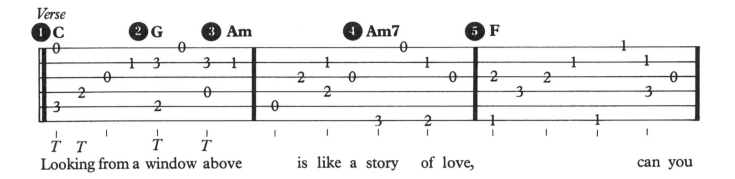

Looking from a window above   is like a story   of love,   can you

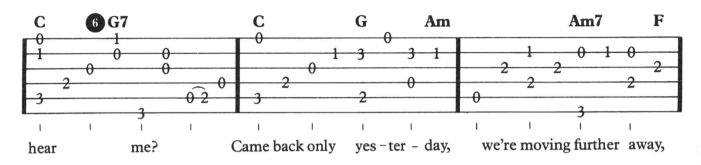

hear   me?   Came back only   yes – ter – day,   we're moving further   away,

Chorus

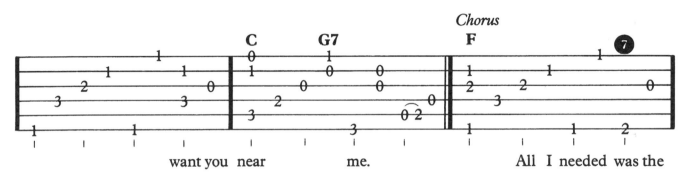

want you near   me.   All I needed was the

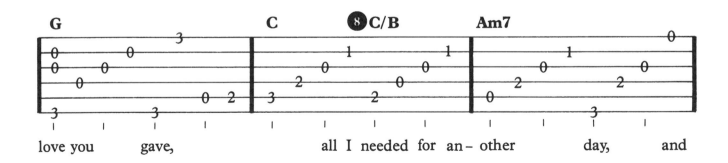

love you   gave,   all I needed for an – other   day,   and

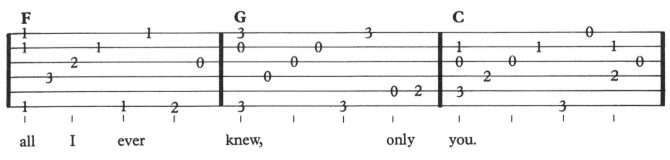

all   I   ever   knew,   only   you.

Only You Continued

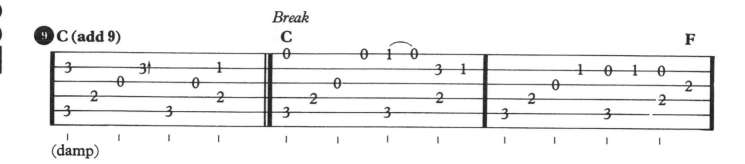

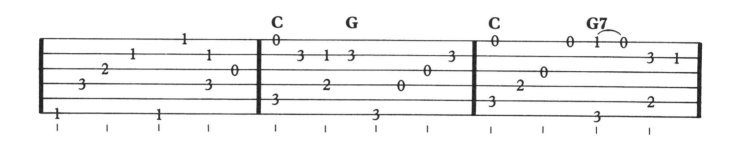

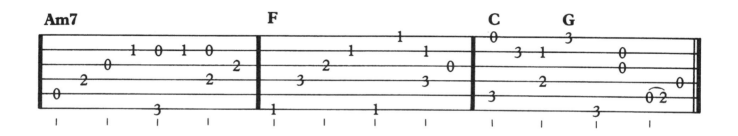

Verse 2:
Sometimes when I think of her name
When it's only a game
And I need you
Listen to the words that you say
It's getting harder to stay
When I see you

Verse 3:
This is gonna take a long time
And I wonder what's mine
Can't take no more
Wonder if you'll understand
It's just the touch of your hand
Behind closed door.

The Boxer Paul Simon

This is a close transcription of Paul Simon's playing in one of his live performances. The alternating thumb style is used mostly, with some bass-strum patterns in the chorus.

The chords are simple, but embellishments are added to them to create an interesting accompaniment.

The piece begins with the usual **C** chord shape, then the 3rd finger moves from the 5th to the 6th string (as shown in the 1st photo). Chords that aren't shown are the usual ones you've seen before. In the 7th bar of the verse, use your 4th finger to hammer on for the G7 chord. Leave your 2nd finger on the 4th string.

1 **C** chord (**g** bass)

2 **C** chord (**b** bass)

3 **G** chord

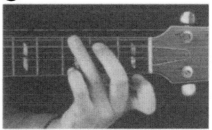

4 **G6** chord

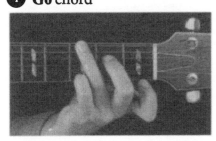

5 **F6** chord

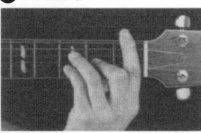

6 **b** and **d** notes

7 **a** and **c** notes

8 **f** note (onto **C** chord)

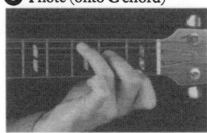

9 **C7** chord

The Boxer Continued

Verse

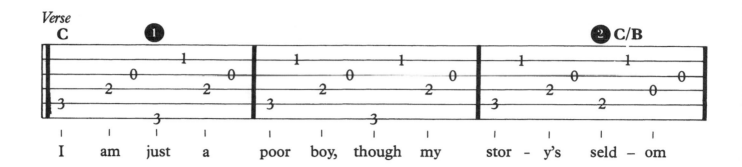

I am just a poor boy, though my stor – y's seld – om

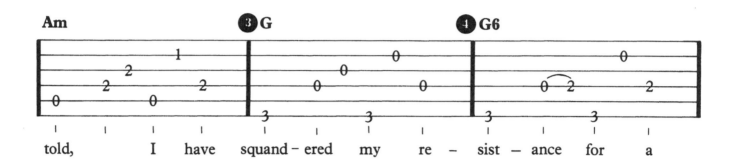

told, I have squand – ered my re – sist – ance for a

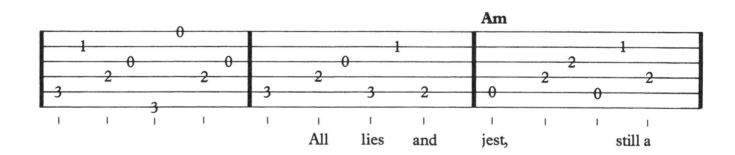

pock – et full of mum – bles such are prom – is – es.

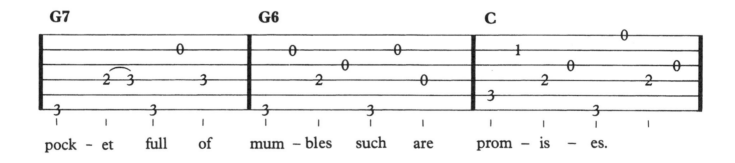

All lies and jest, still a

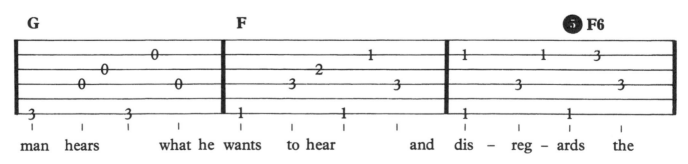

man hears what he wants to hear and dis – reg – ards the

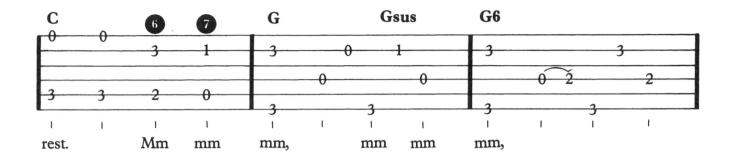

rest.   Mm   mm   mm,   mm   mm   mm,

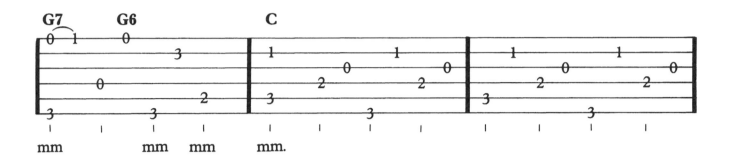

mm   mm   mm   mm.

[*Rpt.* 1st 16 Bars of   *Verse 2 Ending*
verse for Verse 2]   **G**

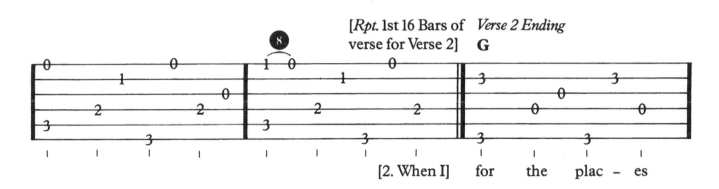

[2. When I]   for   the   plac – es

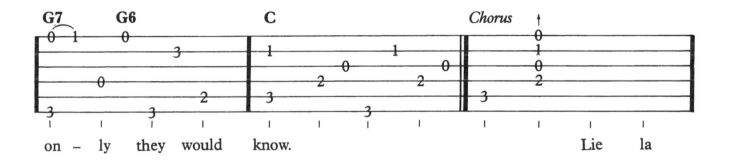

on – ly   they   would   know.   Lie   la

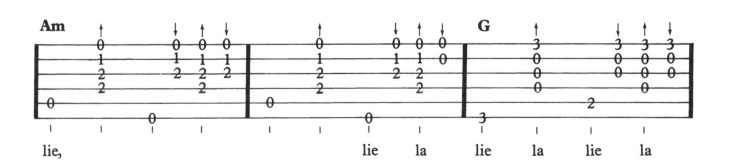

lie,   lie   la   lie   la   lie   la

The Boxer Continued

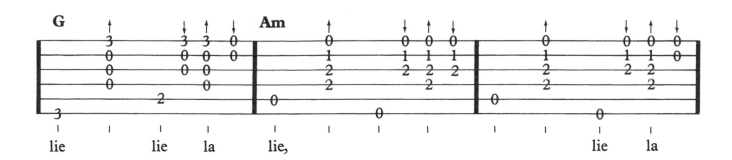

lie   lie   la   lie,   lie   la

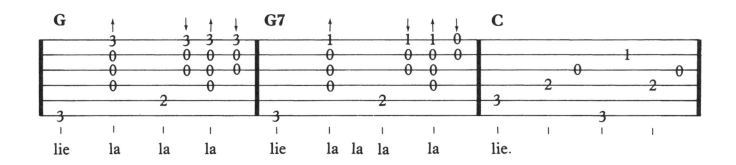

lie   la   la   la   lie   la la la   la   lie.

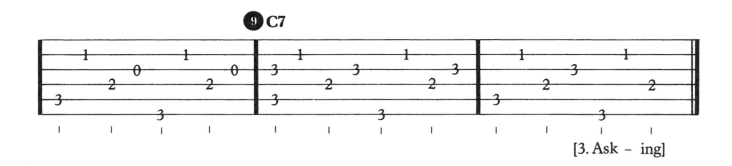

[3. Ask – ing]

Verse 4 Ending [after 8 bars per Verse 1)

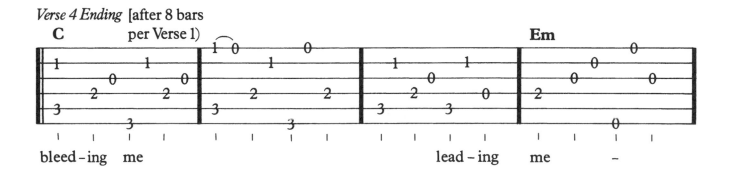

bleed – ing   me   lead – ing   me   –

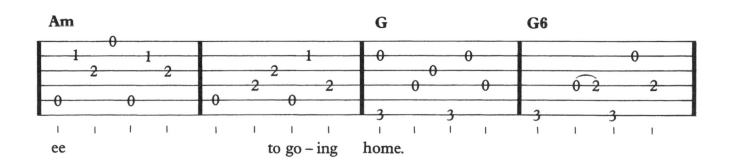

ee   to go – ing   home.

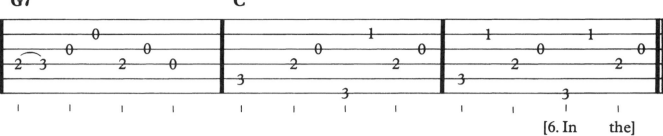

[6. In   the]

Verse 2:
When I left my home and my family I was no
more than a boy
In the company of strangers, in the quiet of a
railway station
Running scared, laying low
Seeking out the poorer quarters where the
ragged people go
Looking for the places only they would know.

Verse 3:
Asking only workman's wages I came looking for
a job
But I got no offers, just a come-on from the
whores
On Seventh Avenue, I do declare
There were times when I was so lonesome I took
some comfort there
Oo la la la la la la la la la.

Verse 4:
Then I'm laying out my winter clothes and
wishing I was gone
Going home where the New York City winters
aren't bleeding me
Leading me to going home.

Verse 5:
Now the years are rolling by me, they are rocking
evenly
And I am older than I once was, and younger
than I'll be
That's not unusual, no it isn't strange
After changes upon changes we are more or less
the same.
After changes we are more or less the same.

Verse 6:
In the clearing stands a boxer and a fighter by his
trade
And he carries the reminders of every glove that
laid him down
Or cut him till he cried out, in his anger and his
shame
"I am leaving, I am leaving," but the fighter still
remains.

59

At The Zoo   Russ Shipton

This piece requires a lot of left hand manoeuvring. The **D, G** and **G7** chords are the usual shapes and are not shown in the photos. Most of the other positions have been shown.

The thumb is used for the **F maj7** chord because this makes the fingering easier overall. The little finger is added for the **d** notes. Raise your 3rd finger for the **g** note on the 6th string as you've done before for the **C** chord in the 4th and last bars.

The 3rd bar from the end has a moving bass line as well as a changing melody on the treble strings. Your 2nd finger should take the **b** note (2nd fret, 5th string), and the 4th finger should

then take the **g** note (3rd fret, 1st string), sliding up for the **a** note as well. The 1st finger should now be in place for the **g** note. The open strings will then give the 1st finger enough time to take the **c** note (1st fret, 2nd string) again.

This is an alternating thumb arrangement, and as usual, all the notes on the beat are struck by the right hand thumb. Don't go too fast for this piece; try to make the notes clear even though you are moving positions quickly.

The **G7** chord halfway through should be played with a 'spread strum' i.e. not like the usual strum which is done quickly, but spread out a little.

❶ C chord (with **high g**)

❷ F chord (**add high c**)

❸ G chord (**add a**)

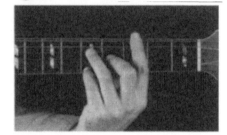

❹ Fmaj7 chord

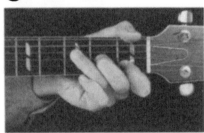

❺ Dadd9 chord (**f♯ bass**)

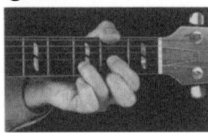

❻ a note (then **g**)

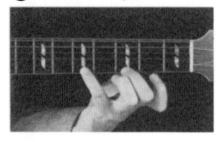

❼ F chord

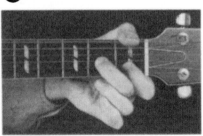

❽ D7 chord

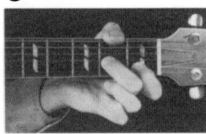

❾ G6 chord

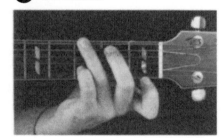

At The Zoo Continued

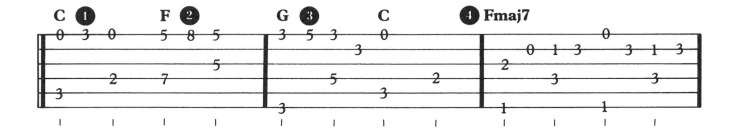

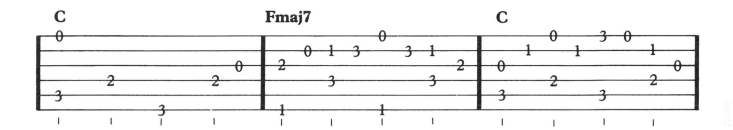

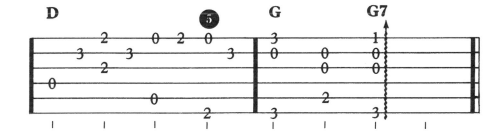

Repeat the first 5 bars

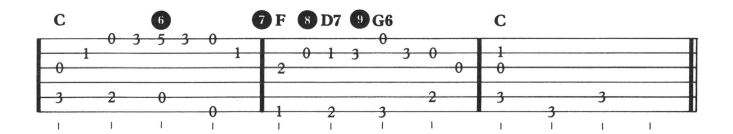

Sixteen Tons   Merle Travis

Slide your 1st and 3rd fingers along two frets to the position shown in the first photo. The next positions are shown in the following photos. The **Am** and **Dm** chords are the usual shapes. Other chords are shown.

This is an alternating thumb arrangement, and the right hand thumb should play all the bass notes on the beat. These should be played firmly for this kind of song. One way to strengthen the rhythm is to damp the bass notes with the heel of your right hand as the thumb plays them. Drop your hand down towards the strings near the bridge. The notes don't have to be completely muted, just partially. Experiment

with this technique because it will give the rhythm more bite – appropriate for a forceful, bluesy song like this one.

The rhythm should involve a 'swing.' See my notes on page 3.

The 2 beat bar is nothing to worry about – just count 1 & 2, and then go on to the next full bar as normal.

Let the final **Am** chord ring on through the two bars at the end.
Play this song steadily with a pronounced beat.

1 **a** notes
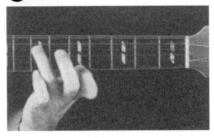

2 **e** notes
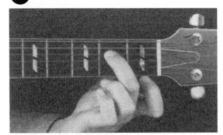

3 **c** notes

4 **a** notes
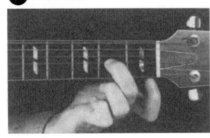

5 **f♯** and **g♯** notes
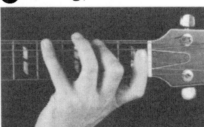

6 **F7** chord
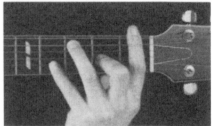

7 **F6** chord
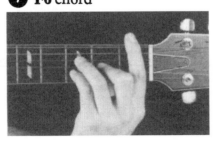

8 **Am7** chord

9 **Am** chord
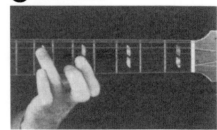

Sixteen Tons Continued

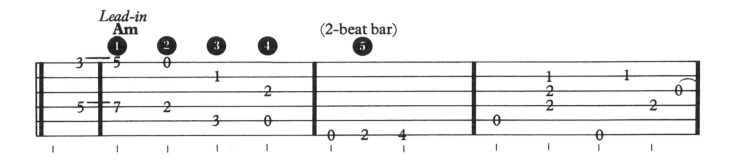

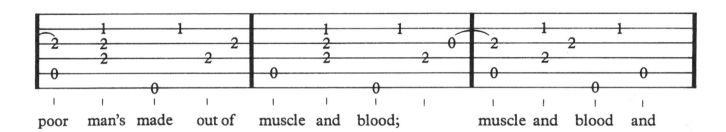

Some people say a man is made out of mud. A

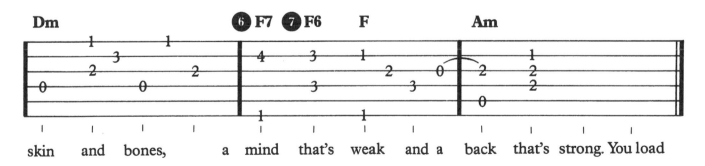

poor man's made out of muscle and blood; muscle and blood and

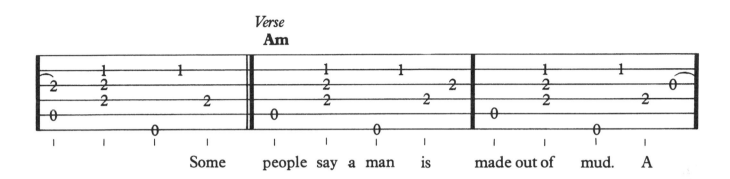

skin and bones, a mind that's weak and a back that's strong. You load

Chorus

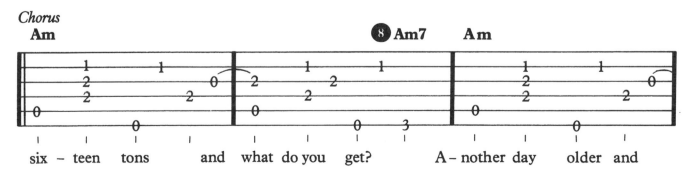

six – teen tons and what do you get? A – nother day older and

Sixteen Tons Continued

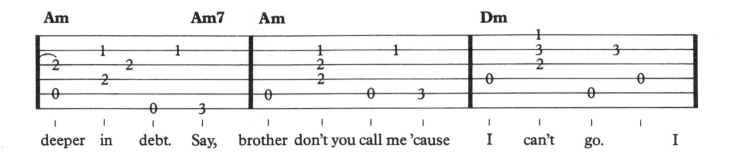

deeper in debt. Say, brother don't you call me 'cause I can't go. I

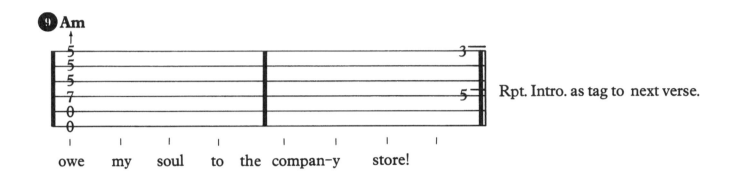

owe my soul to the compan-y store!

Rpt. Intro. as tag to next verse.

Verse 2:
I was born one morning when the sun didn't
shine
I picked up my shovel and I walked to the mine
I loaded sixteen tons of number nine coal
And the straw boss said "Well, a-bless my soul."

Verse 3:
I was born one morning, it was drizzling rain
Fighting and trouble are my middle name
I was raised in a canebrake by an old mama lion
Cain't no high-toned woman make me walk the
line.

Verse 4:
If you see me coming, brother, step aside
A lotta men didn't, a lotta men died
One fist of iron, the other of steel
If the right one don't a-get you, then the left one
will.

Here Comes The Sun George Harrison

George Harrison used the flatpick and the strumming style for this song, with a second guitar to fill out the accompaniment. This alternating thumb arrangement combines both parts and, though the chords are all at the end of the fingerboard, is occasionally quite difficult.

Keep the bass notes nice and steady and count the syncopated bars carefully. The right hand thumb strikes are marked to make them easier to follow.

The 1st 4 bars of the middle section can be repeated several times. Don't worry about the bars – keep tapping the beats.

1 D chord

2 E9 chord

3 E7 chord

4 G6 chord

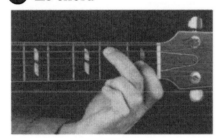

5 A (run)

6 A7sus 4 chord

7 E7 chord

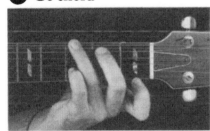

8 c♯ and **e** notes

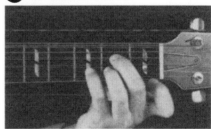

9 F chord

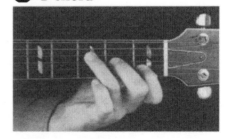

10 C chord

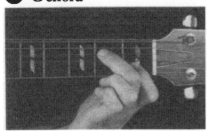

11 G chord

12 A7 chord

Here Comes The Sun Continued

Chorus

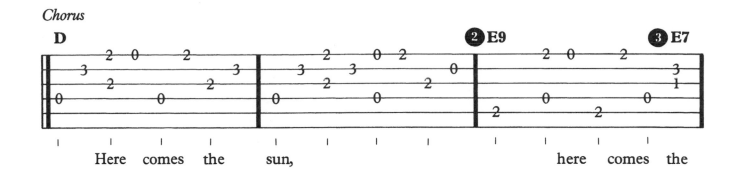

Here comes the sun,   here comes the

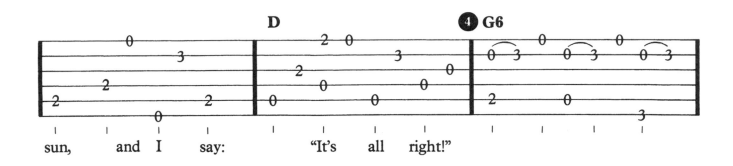

sun,   and I say: "It's all right!"

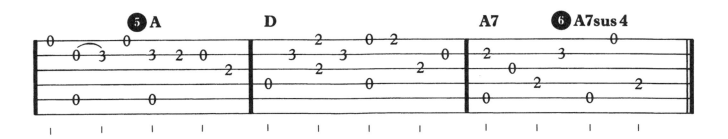

Verse

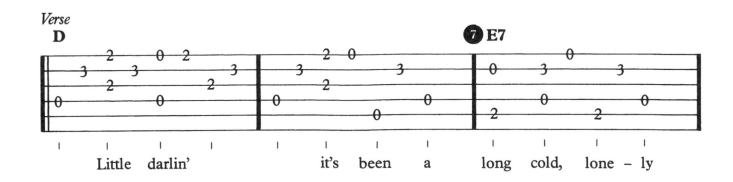

Little darlin'   it's been a   long cold, lone – ly

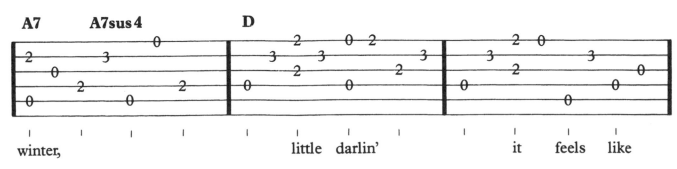

winter,   little darlin'   it feels like

E9   A7

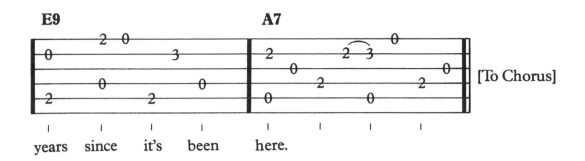

[To Chorus]

years   since   it's   been   here.

Middle Section   (Rpt. 4 bars twice more.)

D   A7 (2-beat bar)   ⑧ ⑨ F   ⑩ C   ⑪ G (3-beat bar)

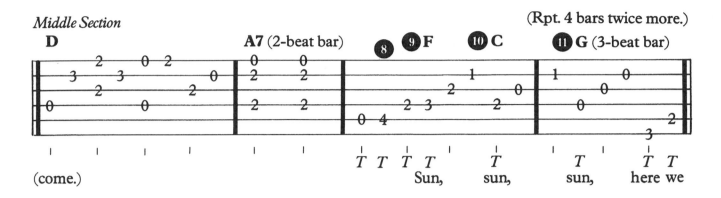

(come.)   Sun,   sun,   sun,   here we

D   A7   A7sus

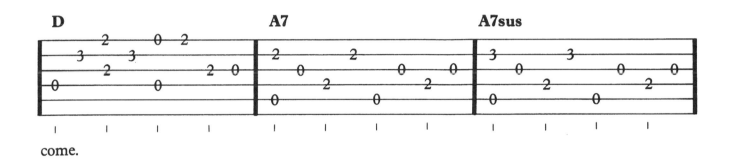

come.

                                Ending

A7   ⑫   (to Verse 3) F   C   G   (2-beat bar) D

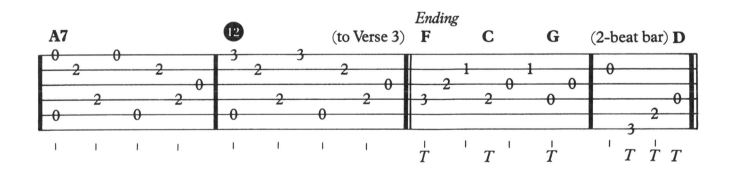

Verse 2:
Little darlin', the smiles returning to their faces
Little darlin', it seems like years since it's been
here.

Verse 3:
Little darlin', I feel that ice is slowly melting
Little darlin', it seems like years since it's been
clear.

Country Slide   Russ Shipton

This instrumental will give you practice with slides, hammer-ons and pull-offs. It involves 'partial' chord shapes that are shown in the photos.

Hold the partial **G** chord (shown in photo 1) one fret lower and slide the **whole** shape up – but striking just the 3rd string. Hammer your 3rd or 4th finger on for the **E** note on the 2nd string. Similarly, you can slide along the whole **G** position shown in the 8th photo, from the 6th to 7th fret. Add your 4th finger to the bar **C, G,** and **A** chords in section 2.

Always look for easier ways of moving from one position to another. The **D** to **D7** in bar 4, for example, could be done using the 2nd, 3rd & 4th fingers for the **D** chord and the 1st finger replacing the 4th to produce the **D7** chord. Try other ways of making changes and choose the one that suits you best.

The tempo should be quite fast once you've learnt the mechanics of the piece.

① G chord

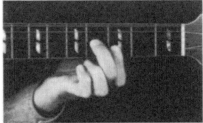

② D chord

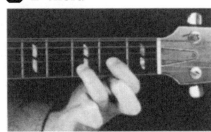

③ D chord

④ D7 chord

⑤ C chord

⑥ C chord

⑦ D chord

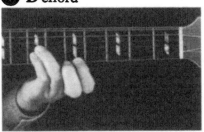

⑧ G chord

⑨ C chord

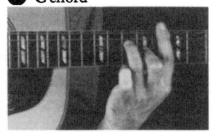

⑩ G chord

⑪ A chord

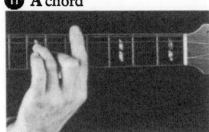

⑫ D7 chord

Country Slide Continued

Section 1

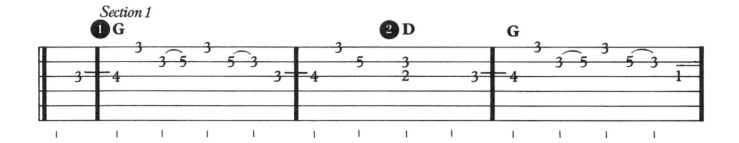

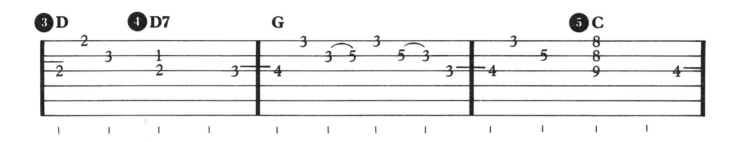

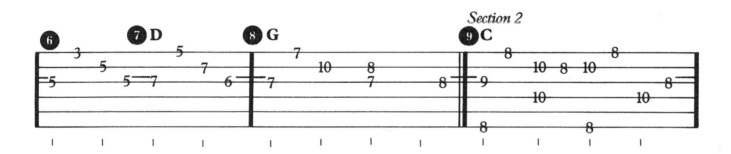

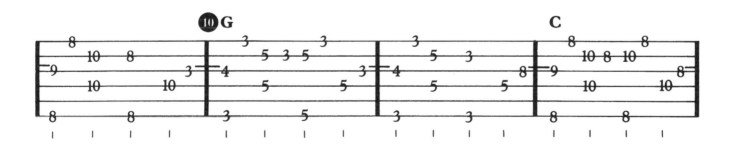

[Rpt. Section 1]

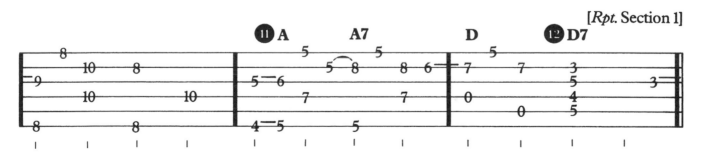

Georgia On My Mind Stuart Gorrell and Hoagy Carmichael

This beautiful melody is blues-based, and the accompaniment includes both the monotonic and alternating thumb right hand styles.

Full chord shapes can be held as shown in the photos, and occasional passing notes are added to them. In certain cases, short "partial" shapes can be used for chords instead of the standard full positions. The **G♯m** in photo 12 for example is part of the full barred **Em** shape. This partial shape could also be used at the 2nd fret for the **F♯m** in the lead-in. Always change the fingering of chords if it makes the playing easier.

Move the 3rd finger from 4th to 5th string for the **G♯7** bar near the start of the chorus. Hold the **D♯7** chord as shown in photo 8, and then move the 3rd finger to the 6th string on the 4th beat of the bar.

Watch out for the chord changes on the half beat, and follow the thumb indications carefully for the lead-in. Count each bar separately, and make sure you don't miss the triplets when they come. This piece does have a triplet feel i.e. a 12/8 or 4 x 3 feel, as do many slow blues songs. Take this song at a slow to medium pace.

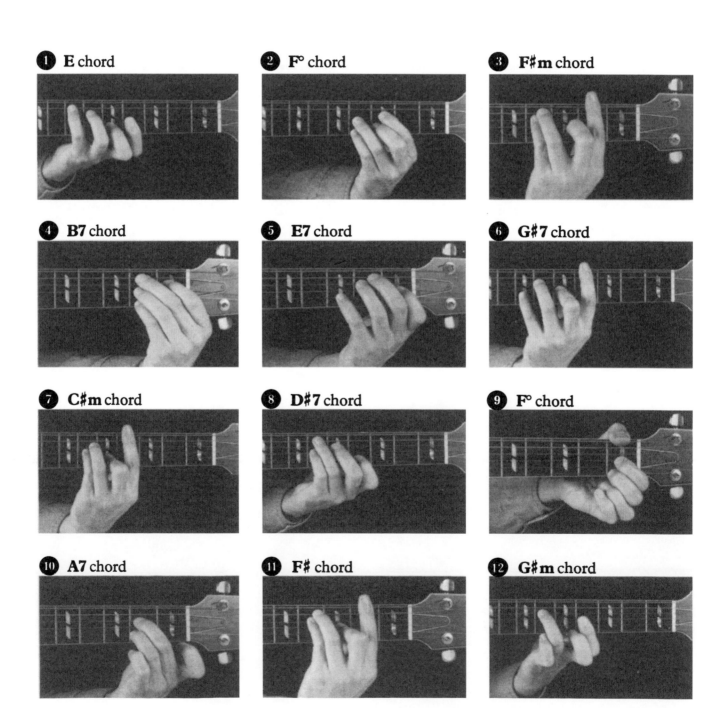

1 **E** chord 2 **F°** chord 3 **F♯m** chord
4 **B7** chord 5 **E7** chord 6 **G♯7** chord
7 **C♯m** chord 8 **D♯7** chord 9 **F°** chord
10 **A7** chord 11 **F♯** chord 12 **G♯m** chord

Georgia On My Mind Continued

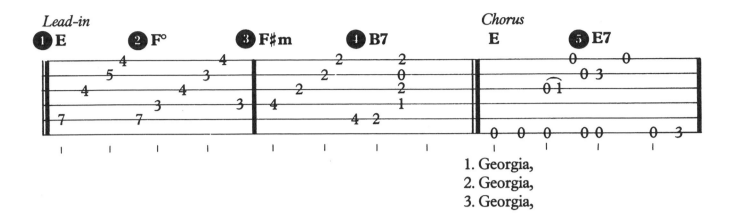

Lead-in

①E   **②F°**   **③F#m**   **④B7**   *Chorus*   **E**   **⑤E7**

1. Georgia,
2. Georgia,
3. Georgia,

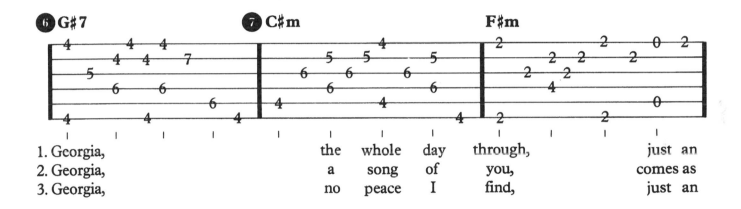

⑥G#7   **⑦C#m**   **F#m**

1. Georgia,   the   whole   day   through,   just an
2. Georgia,   a   song   of   you,   comes as
3. Georgia,   no   peace   I   find,   just an

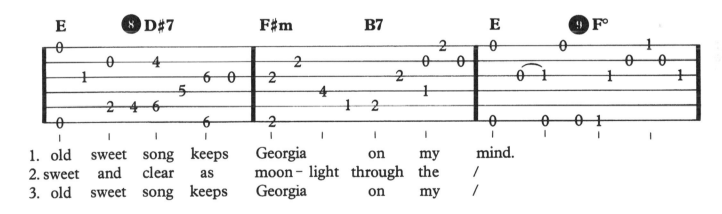

E   **⑧D#7**   **F#m**   **B7**   **E**   **⑨F°**

1. old   sweet   song   keeps   Georgia   on   my   mind.
2. sweet   and   clear   as   moon - light   through   the   /
3. old   sweet   song   keeps   Georgia   on   my   /

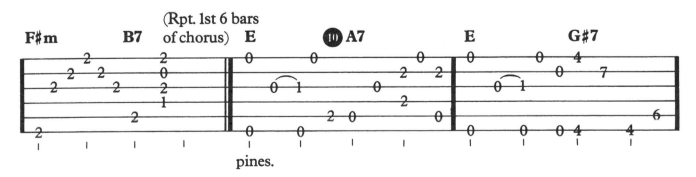

F#m   **B7**   (Rpt. 1st 6 bars of chorus)   **E**   **⑩A7**   **E**   **G#7**

pines.

Georgia On My Mind Continued

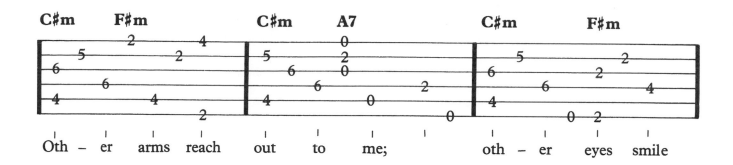

Oth – er arms reach out to me; oth – er eyes smile

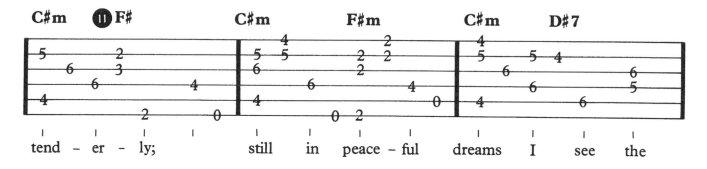

tend – er – ly; still in peace – ful dreams I see the

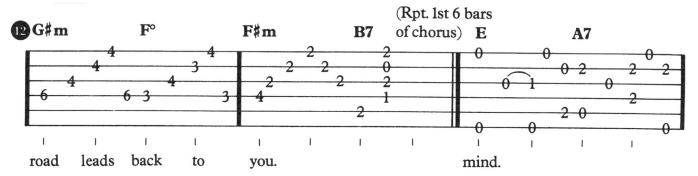

(Rpt. 1st 6 bars of chorus)

road leads back to you. mind.

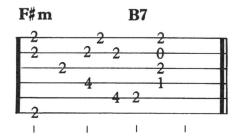

Blackbird   Lennon/McCartney

This is a very clever arrangement which may give the impression of an open tuning sound. In fact it could be done with an open tuning, but this accompaniment follows Paul McCartney's playing quite closely.

Similar shapes are used in different places on the fingerboard – the **C** fingering, for example, is repeated elsewhere as **D, F** and **B,** and the **Em** is **Cm** if you move three frets down. The **A7** in the 5th bar, fingered with the 1st and 2nd fingers becomes a **B7** two frets up. The slide at the start is a little tricky. Use your 2nd and 4th fingers and as you slide them up to their new position, you have to 'spread' them by one fret.

As you can see by the thumb indications, I suggest using your index finger on the right hand for playing the open 3rd string notes for some bars, while using the alternating thumb for others. Experiment and see what you feel happiest doing.

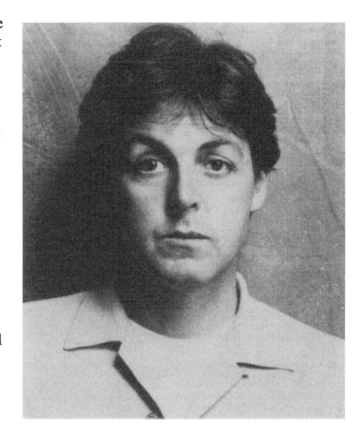

1 G position

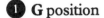

2 Am position

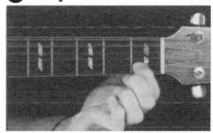

3 G position

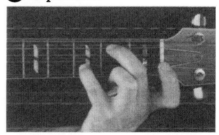

4 G position

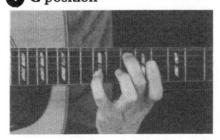

5 C position

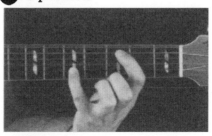

6 Em position

7 Cm position

8 D7 position

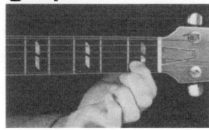

9 B♭ chord

Blackbird Continued

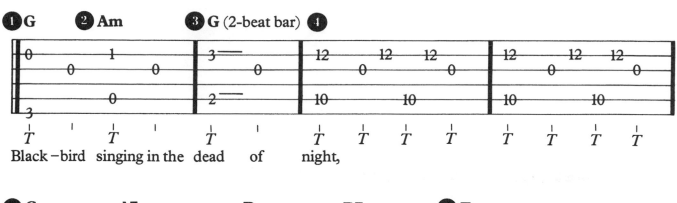

1 G   **2** Am   **3** G (2-beat bar) **4**

Black—bird singing in the dead of night,

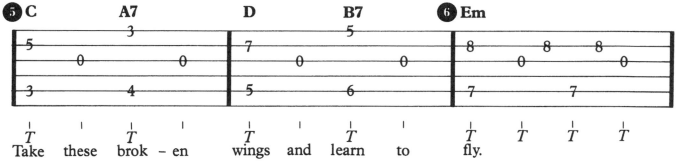

5 C   A7   D   B7   **6** Em

Take these brok – en wings and learn to fly.

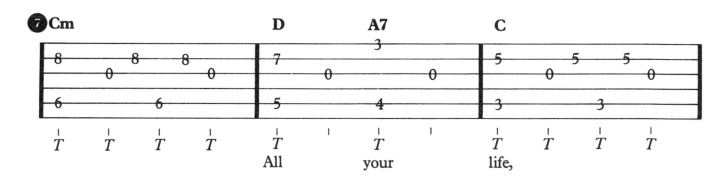

7 Cm   D   A7   C

All your life,

Cm   G   A7

you were on – ly wait – ing for this

Tag

8 D7   G   C   G

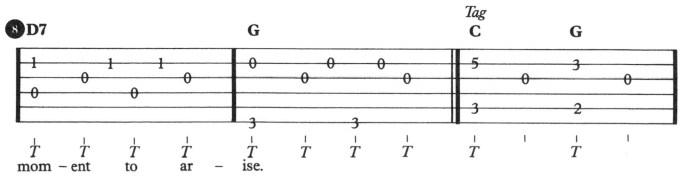

mom – ent to ar – ise.

Middle Section

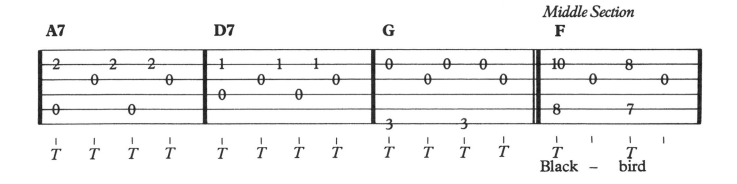

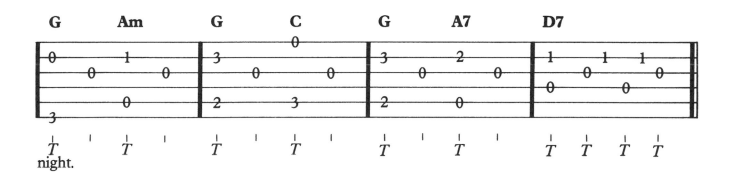

Verse 2:
Blackbird singing in the dead of night
Take these sunken eyes and learn to see
All your life
You were only waiting for this moment to be free.

Fire And Rain James Taylor

James Taylor is the master of syncopation. This arrangement is transcribed from a T.V. performance, and while not looking too difficult, getting it smooth will take you some time.

The chord and shapes are straightforward, but it's the right hand you need to concentrate on. Follow the right hand thumb indications beneath the tablature, and damp (stop the string by releasing the pressure on it) where a 'd' is shown.

The tag on the last page is stressed rather unusually – stress those strums marked with an $<$

1 **A** chord

2 **Em7** chord

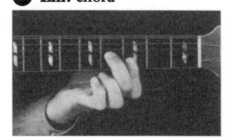

3 **Asus 4** chord

4 **Gmaj7** chord

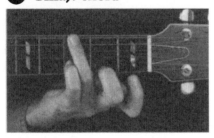

5 **D** chord

6 **E** chord

7 **c#** note

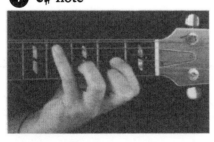

8 **Bm7** chord (**e** bass)

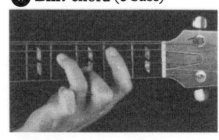

9 **f#** and **a** notes

10 **A add 9** chord

11 **A9** chord

Fire And Rain Continued

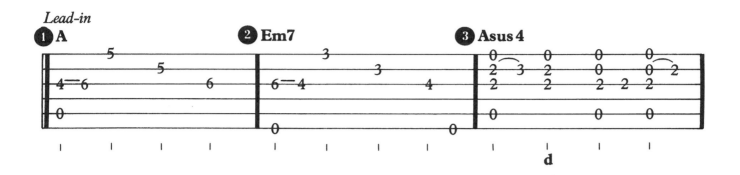

Lead-in
1 A   **2** Em7   **3** Asus 4

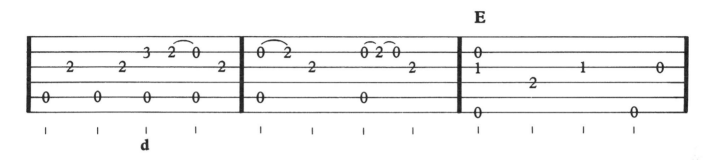

E

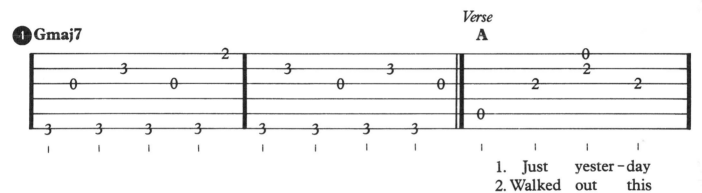

4 Gmaj7   *Verse* A

        1. Just   yester – day
        2. Walked   out   this

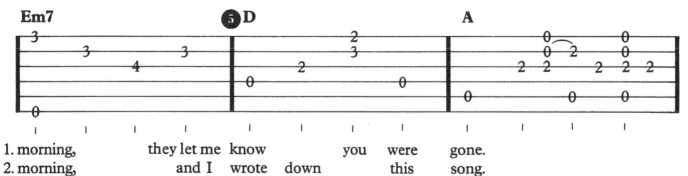

Em7   **5** D   A

1. morning,   they let me know   you   were   gone.
2. morning,   and I   wrote   down   this   song.

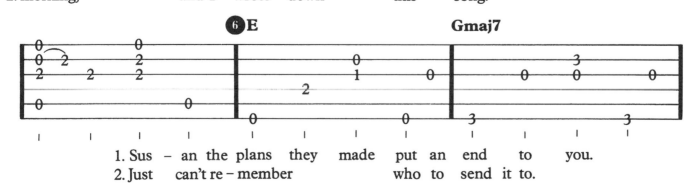

6 E   Gmaj7

1. Sus – an the plans they   made   put an   end   to   you.
2. Just   can't re – member   who to   send it to.

Fire And Rain *Continued*

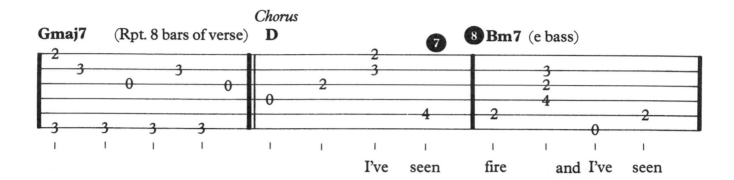

Gmaj7 (Rpt. 8 bars of verse) *Chorus* **D** 7 8 **Bm7** (e bass)

I've seen fire and I've seen

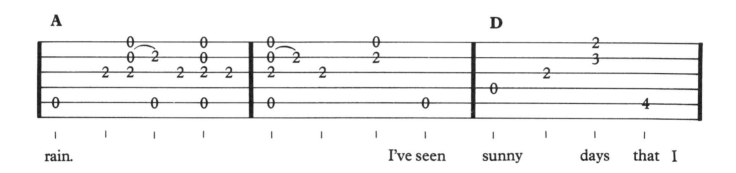

A **D**

rain. I've seen sunny days that I

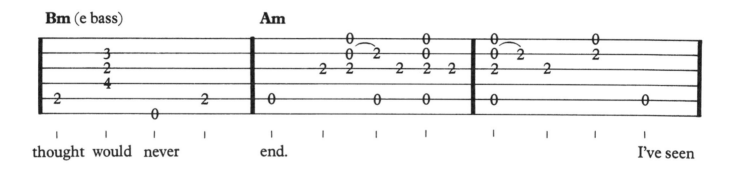

Bm (e bass) **Am**

thought would never end. I've seen

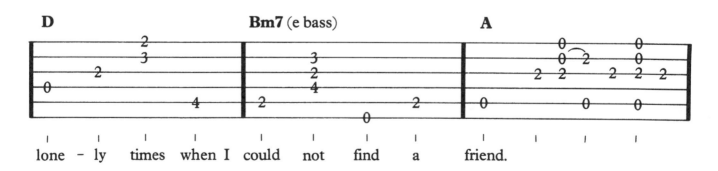

D **Bm7** (e bass) **A**

lone – ly times when I could not find a friend.

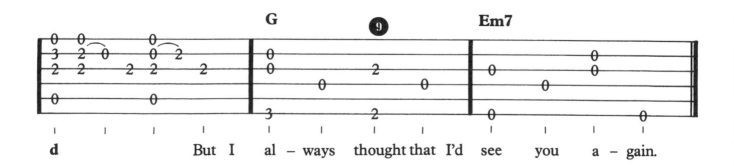

G 9 **Em7**

d But I al – ways thought that I'd see you a – gain.

78

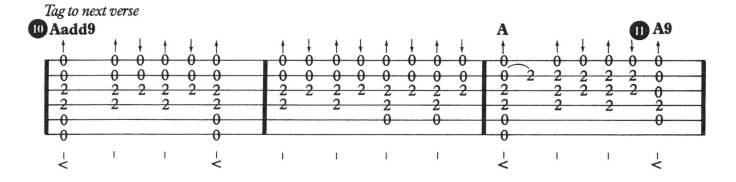

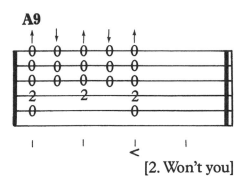

[2. Won't you]

Verse 2:
Won't you look down upon me, Jesus
You've got to help me make a stand
You've just got to see me through another day
My body's aching, and my time is at hand
And I won't make it any other way.

Verse 3:
Now I'm walking my mind to an easy time
My back turned towards the sun
Lord knows when the cold wind blows, it'll turn
your head around
Those hours of time on the telephone line to talk
about things to come
Sweet dreams and flying machines in pieces on
the ground.

Crumble Blues   Russ Shipton

This is another instrumental using partial chord shapes, this time in the blues idiom. Blues in the key of A are very common because open bass strings can be used on the three main chords, **A**, **D**, and **E**.

As we saw in 'Georgia On My Mind', triplets are frequently used in slow blues pieces. You'll also often find bass runs joining the chords.

Experiment with the fingering for these bass runs – using three left hand fingers is probably best.

With blues arrangements you could try dropping the heel of your right hand to damp the bass notes a little. This will take time to master, but it's very useful for strengthening the rhythm.

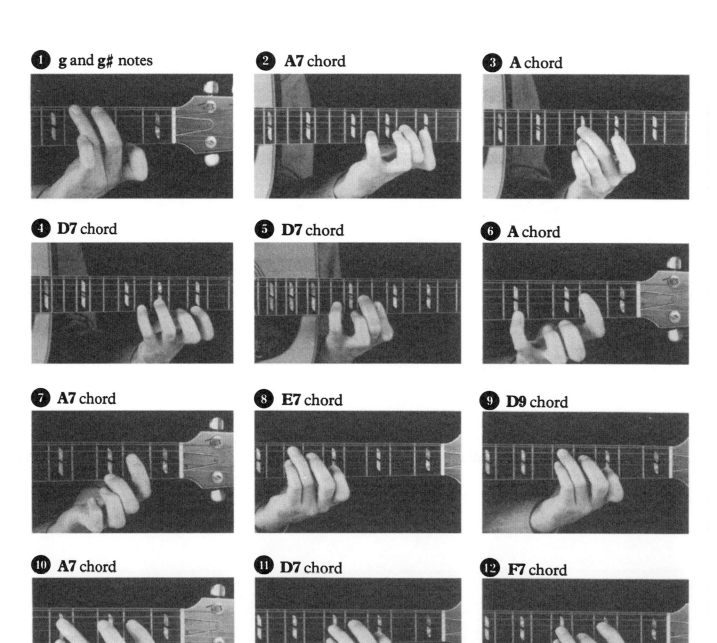

1 **g** and **g#** notes
2 **A7** chord
3 **A** chord
4 **D7** chord
5 **D7** chord
6 **A** chord
7 **A7** chord
8 **E7** chord
9 **D9** chord
10 **A7** chord
11 **D7** chord
12 **F7** chord

Crumble Blues Continued

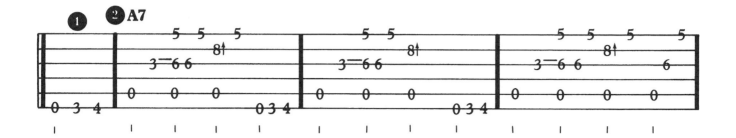

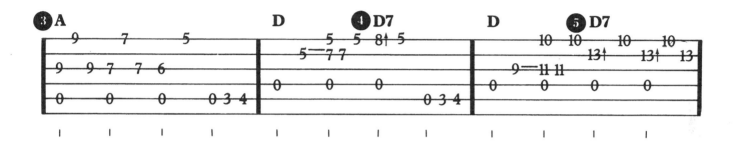

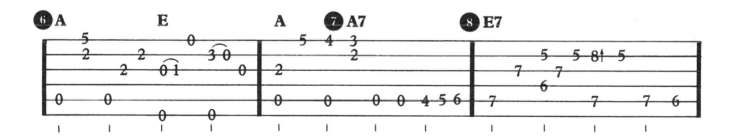

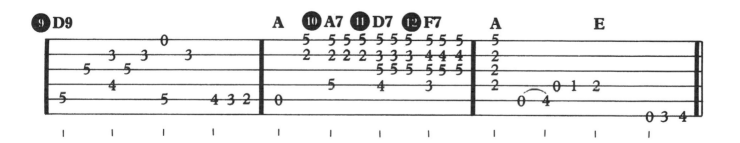

May You Never   John Martyn

This is a very close transcription of John Martyn's early recorded version of this great song. If you want to play along with him, you'll have to put your capo on the 2nd fret. (And lower your 6th string one tone to **d**).

Take each bar individually and slowly, after you've practised a basic 'slap' pattern with just one chord. Your right hand fingers come down onto the strings with a slight tap and they damp them at the same time. These slaps are done only on the 2nd and 4th beats. This produces a rock feel.

In bars 8, 12 & 16, use your 1st finger for the **b** note on the 5th string, and then quickly put it back onto the 3rd string.

1 **F♯m** chord

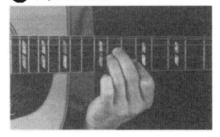

2 **Em** chord (**a** bass)

3 **D** chord

4 **Em7** chord

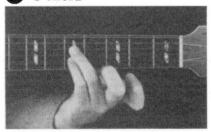

5 **A** chord

6 **Bm7** chord

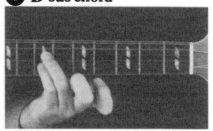

7 **C** chord

8 **D** chord (**add f♯**)

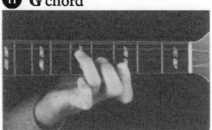

9 **D sus** chord

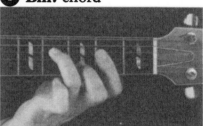

10 **A** chord

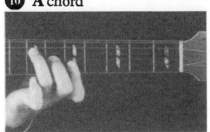

11 **G** chord

12 **a** and **f♯** notes

May You Never Continued

(Tuning: D A D G B E i.e. lower your 6th string one tone to **d**)

Verse

1 F♯m **2 Em** (a bass) **3 D** **4 Em7**

May you nev – er lay your head down, with –

5 A **6 Bm7** **7 C** **D** **Em7**

– out a hand to hold, may you nev – er make your

A **Bm7** **D** **8**

bed up in the cold. You're

A **Bm7** **C** **Bm7** **D**

just like a big, strong brother of mine, and you know that I love you like I

A **Bm7** **C** **Bm7** **D**

should, and you have no knife to stab me in the back, and you

May You Never Continued

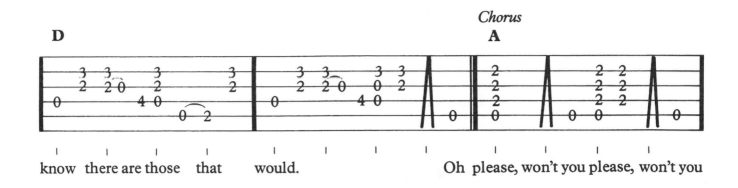

Chorus

know there are those that would.   Oh please, won't you please, won't you

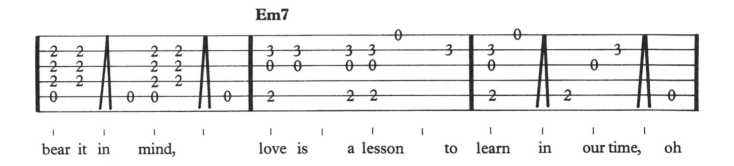

bear it in mind,   love is   a lesson   to learn   in   our time,   oh

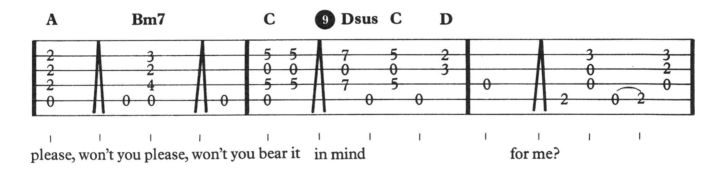

please, won't you please, won't you bear it   in mind   for me?

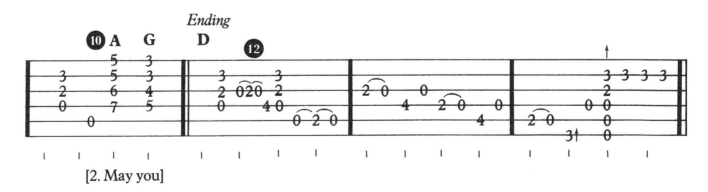

[2. May you]

Verse 2:
May you never lose your temper and get into a
bar-room fight
May you never lose your woman overnight
You're just like a sweet little sister of mine
And you know that I love you true
You never talk dirty behind my back
And I know there are those that do.

Ain't Misbehavin'   Words: Andy Razaf. Music: Thomas Waller and Harry Brooks

There are many chord shapes for you to remember here, but they'll all come in handy for other jazz arrangements. Also, no huge stretches are involved and they're almost all standard jazz shapes. Use the same shape shown for the Em chord in photo 8 for the Am chord in bar 3.

The right hand thumb is 'jumping', as shown under the 1st line. This sometimes means the chord change coming before the next bar begins.

{ means a 'quick arpeggio' by the right hand thumb and three fingers. In this case, the arpeggio starts on the half beat.

1 Cmaj7 chord

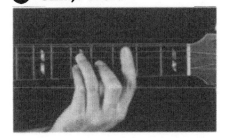

2 C#° chord

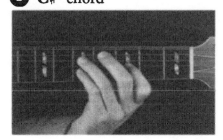

3 Dm7 chord

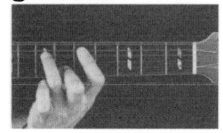

4 D#° chord

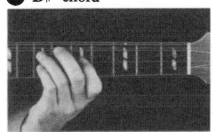

5 Em7 chord

6 F maj 7 chord

7 Fm chord

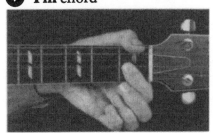

8 Em chord

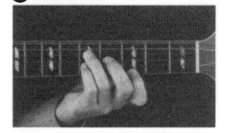

9 A7 chord

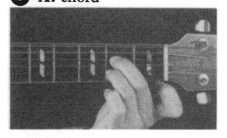

10 Dm7 chord

11 G9 chord

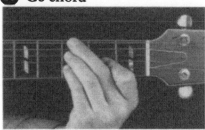

12 G7 chord

13 **C7** chord
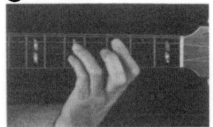

14 **C6** chord

15 **E7** chord

16 **Am7** chord
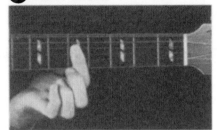

17 **Am6** chord

18 **Am#5** chord

19 **A7** chord
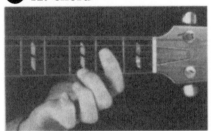

20 **D7** chord

21 **Am7** chord
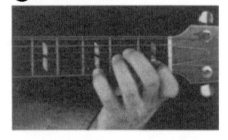

22 **D9** chord
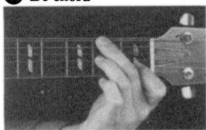

23 **Cmaj7** chord
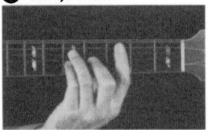

24 **Fmaj7** chord
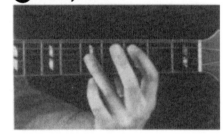

25 **G7sus** chord
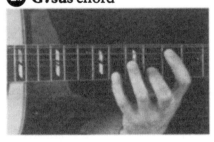

26 **Cmaj7** chord
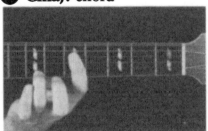

Ain't Misbehavin' Continued

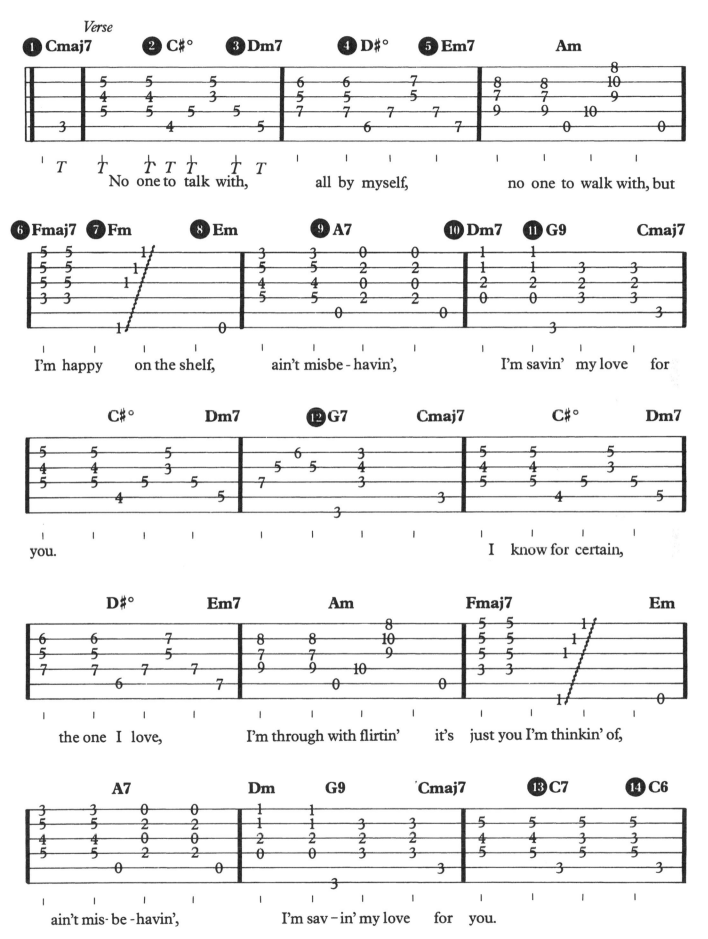

Ain't Misbehavin' Continued

Middle Section

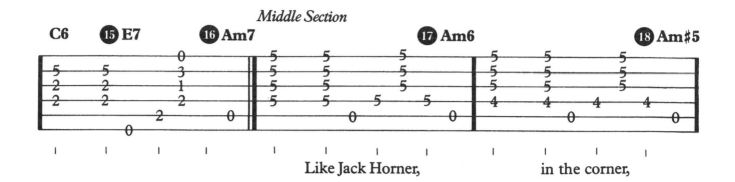

Like Jack Horner,   in the corner,

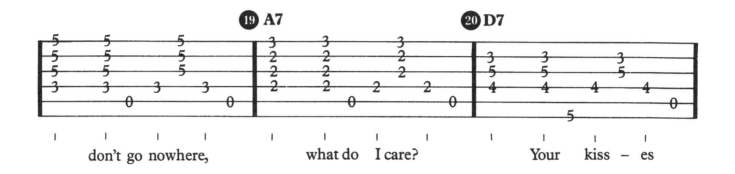

don't go nowhere,   what do I care?   Your   kiss – es

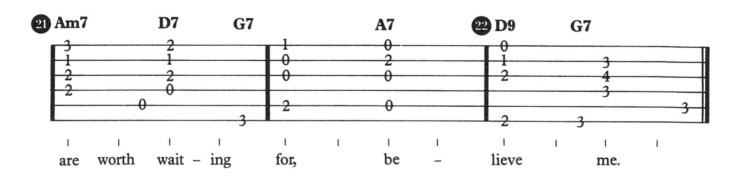

are   worth   wait – ing   for,   be – lieve   me.

Ending

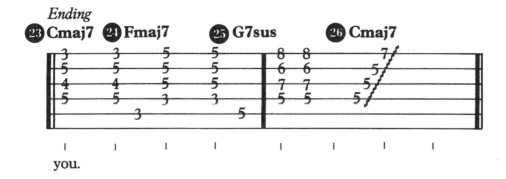

you.

Verse 2:
I don't stay out late
Don't care to go
I'm home about eight
Just me and my radio
Ain't misbehavin'
I'm savin' my love for you.

Everything Put Together Falls Apart Paul Simon

This is transcribed from the record, and is a very interesting arrangement with unusual key changes. Again, there are a lot of positions to remember, but they're not too difficult to finger.

A few slaps with the right hand come into this arrangement. They fill in the rhythm and sound when the melody stops. As in 'Ain't Misbehavin', the right hand thumb bouncing on some chords means a chord change before the start of some bars.

All the slides in this accompaniment are from an 'indeterminate' fret below, except in the penultimate bar. Try sliding from one or two frets below.

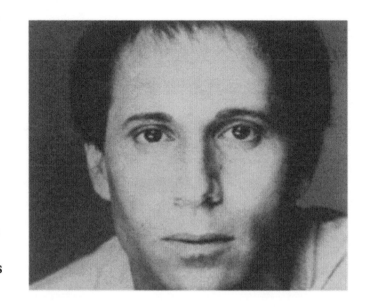

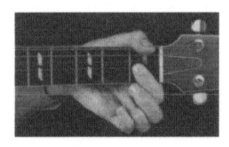

4 **Cm7sus** chord

5 **B♭** chord

6 **B♭** chord (**g** bass)

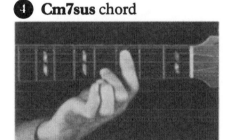

7 **B** chord

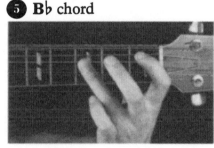

8 **add e** note

9 **add f♯** note

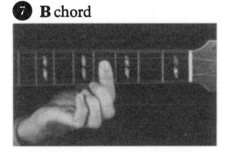

10 **B** chord

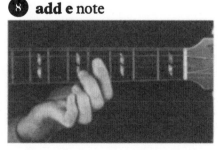

11 **b♭** bass

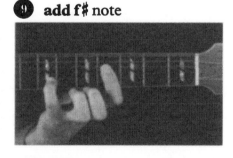

12 **E** chord

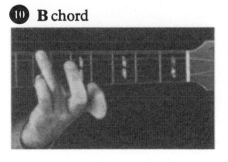

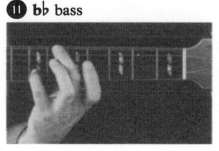

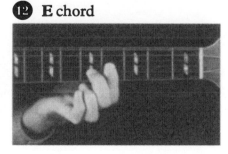

13 **Dmaj7** chord

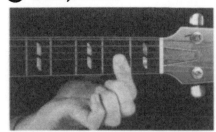

14 **E7** chord

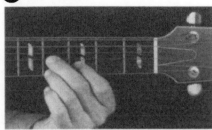

15 **A** chord

16 **Am** chord

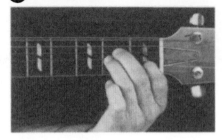

17 **Em** chord

18 **F#m** chord

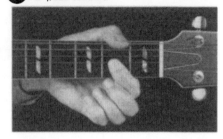

19 **Dm7** chord

20 **Cmaj7** chord

21 **D** chord

22 **Dm** chord

23 **G7** chord

24 **C7** chord

Everything Put Together Falls Apart Continued

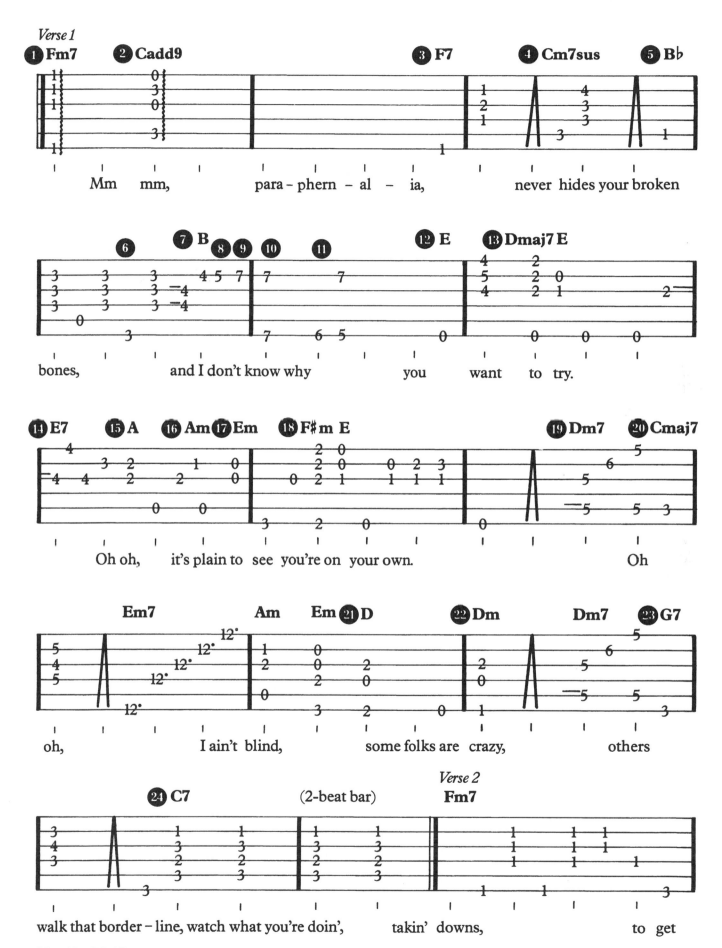

Everything Put Together Falls Apart Continued

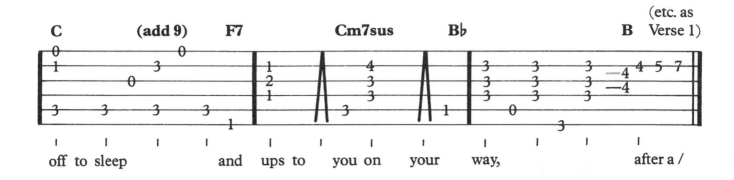

off to sleep   and ups to you on your way,   after a /

Ending

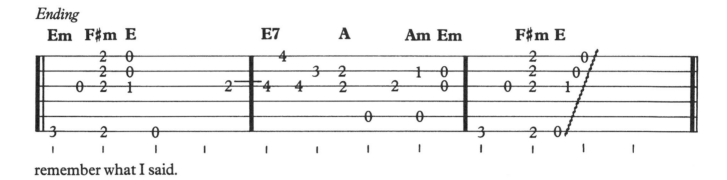

remember what I said.

Verse 2:
Takin' downs to get off to sleep
And ups to start you on your way
After a while, they'll change your style
Mm, mm, I see it happening every day.
Oh oh, spare your heart
Everything put together sooner or later falls apart.
There's nothin' to it, nothin' to it

Verse 3:
You can cry, and you can lie
For all the good it'll do you, you can die
Oh, but when it's done and the police come
And they're layin' you down for dead
Oh oh, just remember what I said.

Sultans of Swing Mark Knopfler

Here is another slap style piece for you to enjoy, though the 3rd finger left hand bar position has to be held quite a lot and your hand will probably get tired. Take frequent rests when you're practising this one!

Mark Knopfler is a great guitarist, but he does have a bit of help from the others in Dire Straits. He doesn't have to fill in all the rhythm. As a solo performance, your two hands have to work very hard.

This arrangement is based on his live performance L.P. track. Follow the photos and rhythm very carefully. Getting the slap steady as well as doing the other notes is not easy.

For the **C** position at the end of the 2nd verse (the bar where you sing 'sound'), just drop your first finger to bar the 5th fret notes and take your other fingers off from the **Dm** position. This is easier than moving quickly down to the **C** position as shown in the photo, and then back again.

❶ Dm chord

❷ C chord

❸ B♭ chord

❹ C sus chord

❺ A chord

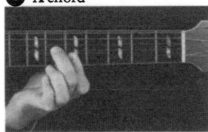

❻ a and **b♭** notes

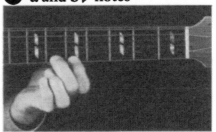

❼ a and **g** notes

❽ F chord

❾ Dm 7 chord (for run)

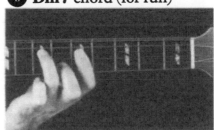

93

Sultans Of Swing Continued

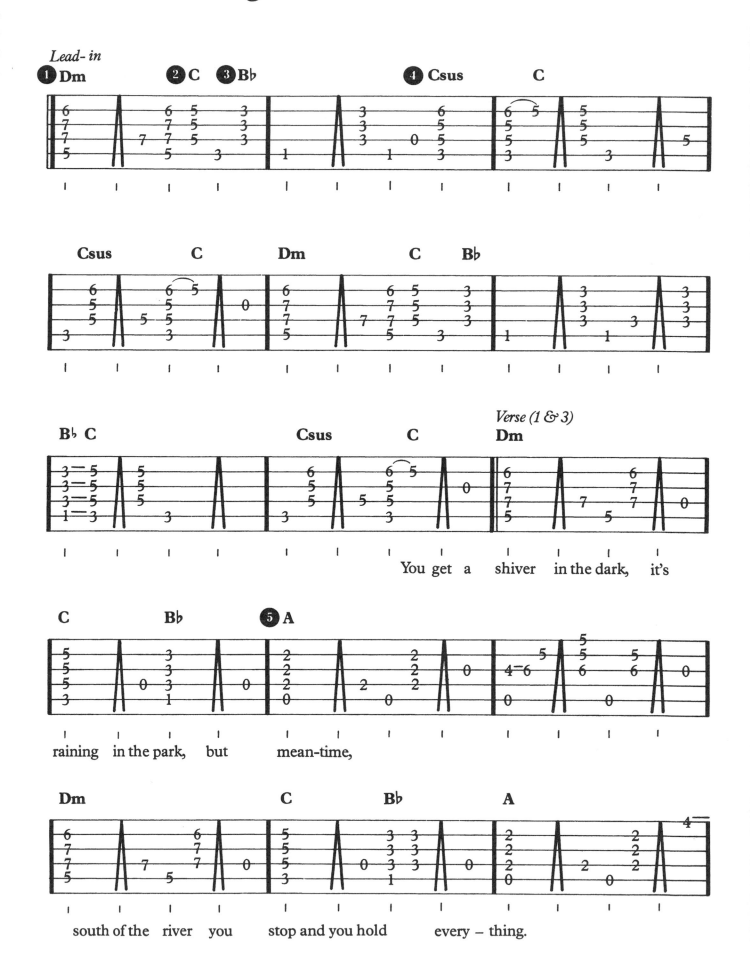

Lead-in

①Dm   **②C ③B♭**   **④Csus**   **C**

Csus   **C**   **Dm**   **C**   **B♭**

B♭ C   **Csus**   **C**   *Verse (1 & 3)* **Dm**

You get a shiver in the dark, it's

C   **B♭**   **⑤A**

raining in the park, but mean-time,

Dm   **C**   **B♭**   **A**

south of the river you stop and you hold every – thing.

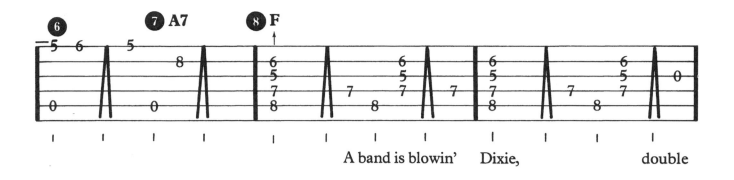

A band is blowin' Dixie,   double

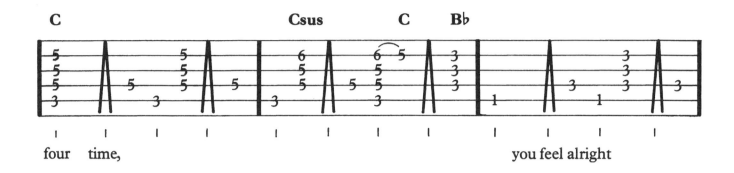

four   time,   you feel alright

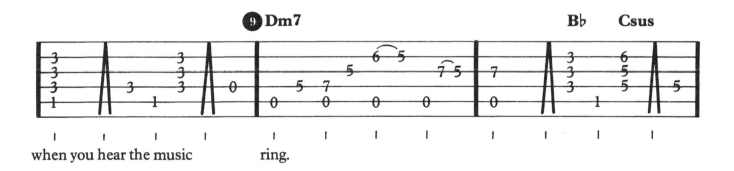

when you hear the music   ring.

End of Verse 2

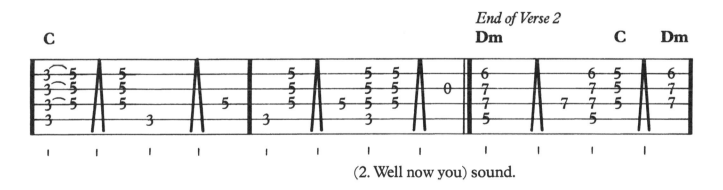

(2. Well now you) sound.

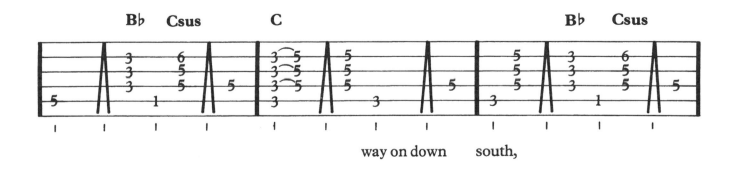

way on down   south,

Level 4

Sultans Of Swing Continued

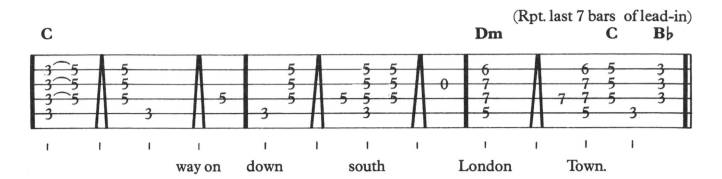

(Rpt. last 7 bars of lead-in)

way on   down   south   London   Town.

Verse 2:
Well now you step inside, but you don't see too
many faces
Comin' in out of the rain to hear the jazz go down
Competition in other places, but the horns,
they're blowin' that sound.
Way on down south, way on down south,
London Town.

Verse 3:
You check out Guitar George, he knows all the
chords
Mind he's strictly rhythm, he doesn't want to
make it cry or sing
This and an old guitar is all he can afford
When he gets up under the lights to play his
thing.

Verse 4:
And Harry doesn't mind if he doesn't make the
scene
He's got a daytime job, he's doin' all right
He can play the honky-tonk like anything
Savin' it up for Friday night with the Sultans,
with the Sultans of Swing.

Verse 5:
And a crowd of young boys, they're foolin'
around in the corner
Drunk and dressed in their best brown baggies
and their platform soles
They don't give a damn about any trumpet
playin' band
It ain't what they call rock and roll
And the Sultans, yeah the Sultans, they played
Creole.

Verse 6:
And then The Man, he steps right up to the
microphone
And says, at last, just as the time-bell rings:
"Good night, now it's time to go home"
And he makes it fast with one more thing:
"We are the Sultans, we are the Sultans of
Swing".